How to Repair Your Credit Score Now:

Simple No Cost Methods You Can Put to Use Today

By
Jamaine Burrell

How To Repair Your Credit Score Now: Simple No Cost Methods You Can Use Today

ISBN-13: 978-0-910627-94-8 ISBN-10: 0-910627-94-0

Library of Congress Cataloging-in-Publication Data

Burrell, Jamaine, 1958-
  How to Repair Your Credit Score NOW: Simple No Cost Methods
You Can Put to Use Today / Author: Jamaine Burrell.
     p. cm.
Includes bibliographical references and index.
ISBN-13: 978-0-910627-94-8 (alk. paper)
ISBN-10: 0-910627-94-0 (alk. paper)
1. Credit scoring systems--United States. 2. Consumer credit--United States.
3. Credit Rating--United States. I. Title.

HG3751.7.B87. .2007
332.7'5--dc22
                                        2007009083

EDITOR: Marie Lujanac • mlujanac817@yahoo.com
PROOFREADER: Vickie Taylor • vtaylor@atlantic-pub.com
ART DIRECTION: Meg Buchner • megadesn@mchsi.com

Printed on Recycled Paper

Printed in the United States

We recently lost our beloved pet "Bear," who was not only
our best and dearest friend but also the "Vice President of
Sunshine" here at Atlantic Publishing. He did not receive
a salary but worked tirelessly 24 hours a day to please
his parents. Bear was a rescue dog that turned around
and showered myself, my wife Sherri, his grandparents
Jean, Bob and Nancy and every person and animal he met
(maybe not rabbits) with friendship and love. He made a
lot of people smile every day.

We wanted you to know that a portion of the profits of this
book will be donated to The Humane Society of
the United States.

–Douglas & Sherri Brown

THE HUMANE SOCIETY
OF THE UNITED STATES ©

The human-animal bond is as old as human history. We cherish our animal companions for their unconditional affection and acceptance. We feel a thrill when we glimpse wild creatures in their natural habitat or in our own backyard.

Unfortunately, the human-animal bond has at times been weakened. Humans have exploited some animal species to the point of extinction.

The Humane Society of the United States makes a difference in the lives of animals here at home and worldwide. The HSUS is dedicated to creating a world where our relationship with animals is guided by compassion. We seek a truly humane society in which animals are respected for their intrinsic value, and where the human-animal bond is strong.

Want to help animals? We have plenty of suggestions. Adopt a pet from a local shelter, join The Humane Society and be a part of our work to help companion animals and wildlife. You will be funding our educational, legislative, investigative and outreach projects in the U.S. and across the globe.

Or perhaps you'd like to make a memorial donation in honor of a pet, friend or relative? You can through our Kindred Spirits program. And if you'd like to contribute in a more structured way, our Planned Giving Office has suggestions about estate planning, annuities, and even gifts of stock that avoid capital gains taxes.

Maybe you have land that you would like to preserve as a lasting habitat for wildlife. Our Wildlife Land Trust can help you. Perhaps the land you want to share is a backyard—that's enough. Our Urban Wildlife Sanctuary Program will show you how to create a habitat for your wild neighbors.

So you see, it's easy to help animals. And The HSUS is here to help.

The Humane Society of the United States
2100 L Street NW
Washington, DC 20037
202-452-1100
www.hsus.org

CONTENTS

CHAPTER 3: CREDIT SCORING MODELS   81

CHAPTER 4: BUILDING CREDIT   97

CHAPTER 5: REPAIRING BAD CREDIT 133

CHAPTER 6: CONSUMER CREDIT COUNSELING   179

CHAPTER 7: IDENTITY THEFT   191

CHAPTER 8: FILING BANKRUPTCY   201

CHAPTER 9: MAINTAINING GOOD CREDIT   227

FOREWORD

By Hazel B. Valera
President and CEO
Clear Credit Exchange

In my work with credit challenged businesses and individuals, the subject of bad credit strikes an emotional chord with most of my clients. They find it difficult to ask for help because they think it means admitting that they have failed to manage a basic indicator of success in America. With more people than ever before filing for bankruptcy and with the economy fluctuating at rates unheard of since 1929, this new book, How to Repair Your Credit Score Now, is timely, not only for its subject matter, but for correcting and upgrading credit scores. Not everyone can afford a professional to dig through the morass that is credit reporting in the 21st Century.

After working with hundreds of clients, I have found that people have the power to rebuild their credit on their own. All they lack is the confidence and the information. This book empowers people with information, giving them the tools they need to help themselves. It makes use of the latest technologies and the most up-to-date methods for fixing cracks in your credit so that you can get back on the road to success. Using this book as a guide, you will learn the tools to recover from bad credit on your own. As a certified debt arbitrator and credit coach, I have witnessed the joy that comes with attaining a good credit rating, when financial self-esteem goes from "worthless" to "priceless." This is something that you can attain simply by heeding the logical credit repair phases offered in this book.

Hazel B. Valera
President and CEO , Clear Credit Exchange
O: 408-868-4272 F: 408-877-1555
E: clearcredit@comcast.net
W: **www.clearcreditexchange.com**

Valera is a former mortgage and real estate professional with more than 14 years of real estate finance, underwriting, and foreclosure experience. Her history also includes the successful operation and management of two credit reporting companies in California. Hazel serves as a credit advisor to many real estate investment firms, mortgage brokers, and executives nationwide, and is a trusted expert in her field.

Sponsored by many title companies nationwide, Valera is a known speaker in the real estate and credit industry and holds regular real estate training classes for loan officers on how to extend assistance to credit challenged clients instead of turning them away.

Valera's mission is to inspire and empower people through financial and credit education.

INTRODUCTION

Repairing your credit score involves an understanding of the parameters that are used to calculate your credit score and taking the necessary actions to manipulate those parameters to work in your favor.

As a consumer your first responsibility in repairing your credit score is to ensure that it was calculated from accurate information describing your credit activities.

By being a U.S. citizen, your financial activity is documented, stored, and maintained in consumer files that are sold and distributed. Contrary to common beliefs, the government does not carry out this transmission of your personal and financial information; private companies do. No one asks whether you want to establish a consumer file. It is created without your knowledge. Further, you can do nothing to prevent companies from compiling this information. Companies and individuals with whom you have financial transactions are responsible for reporting information about those transactions to consumer reporting agencies on your behalf. You will not have an opportunity to approve or disapprove the information, but you must deal with the consequences of having the information in your consumer file.

The information may be inaccurate or just plain wrong. It may belong in someone else's consumer file with the same or a similar name, address, social security number, or other personal information.

Inaccurate data may spawn a variety of different profiles for you that will affect your ability to perform any financial transaction.

Of the various consumer files that are compiled, maintained, and sold about you, credit files are held by credit reporting agencies, particularly the big three: Equifax, TransUnion, and Experian. The information in these files is used to calculate a credit profile and credit score describing you financially. Other companies also compile information about transactions you engage in that involve money, such as renting property, gambling, applying for employment, acquiring insurance, applying for a promotion, opening bank accounts, and being billed medically. While much personal financial information is compiled and sold about you, you are not entitled to know how these companies generate the profiles or credit scores specific to you. The methodology used by these companies is proprietary. Information reported about you by companies and individuals is not the only information included in consumer files used to profile you and calculate your credit score. Information is also acquired from public records as reported by courts and other entities of the government. This information may also be wrong.

While you may know nothing about the companies that compile such information about you or how they operate, your personal and financial information is an open book for them to sell. The federal government has established the Fair Credit and Reporting Act (FCRA), which justifies the existence of these companies and attempts to regulate how they use the information and how they are to restrict access to confidential information. The FCRA gives you the right to examine your credit file and establishes procedures that you may follow to remove or correct entries in your file that are negative, incorrect, or outdated. The FCRA also grants access only to those businesses and entities that have a permissible purpose. An amendment to the FCRA, the Fair and Accurate Credit Transaction Act (FACT Act), extends the scope of regulations established for credit reporting agencies to all other types of consumer reporting agencies. The FACT Act attempts to set standards that all consumer reporting agencies must meet or be liable for damages.

This book will introduce you to the various types of consumer files about you and explain how to get copies of those files and how to have incorrect information removed as the first step in improving your credit score. It will also explain what credit is, the different types of credit, and how credit affects your credit rating and credit score. It will detail the most common types of public records that affect your credit rating and score, and it reveals how certain life events may affect your ability to acquire and maintain credit accounts that affect your credit score.

Chapter One, "What is a Credit Score?," will tell you how to obtain your credit score and its significance. It defines obligations, rights, and responsibilities specified by the FCRA and the FACT Act. It differentiates a credit score from a credit report from a credit file. Further, it defines a credit-reporting agency and other types of consumer reporting agencies, and it explains how to get copies of your consumer files and reports.

Chapter Two, "The Credit Report," outlines parts of a credit report, specifically those public records and collection accounts that do the most damage to your credit rating. It tells you how long entries may remain in your report, and it identifies information that must be excluded from it.

Chapter Three, "Credit Scoring Models," discusses the Fair Isaac Corporationoration (FICO) scoring model and other credit scoring models that are used in the credit industry. It outlines the parameters used in scoring models. This chapter also discusses credit risks and credit risk predictions.

Chapter Four, "Building Credit," tells you which credit accounts will assist in building credit as well as those accounts that do nothing to assist in building credit. This chapter discusses how certain life events, such as marriage, divorce, or enrolling in college may affect your ability to establish credit. It also shows you how to perform debt calculations the same way a lender does.

Chapter Five, "Repairing Bad Credit," explores the consequences of having bad credit, credit rejection, and adverse actions against credit accounts. This chapter defines the steps necessary to repair bad credit. It includes how to find and correct errors and omissions, how to establish a credit repair plan, how to establish a dialogue with creditors, and how to deal with debt collectors, as well as listing what they may and may not do. It outlines how to file suit against creditors, credit reporting agencies, and debt collectors that maintain incorrect information about you.

Chapter Six, "Consumer Credit Counseling," discusses consumer credit counseling agencies, the services they offer, and how to contact them for assistance. This chapter also gives you an in-depth look at detecting consumer credit counseling scams.

Chapter Seven, "Identity Theft," goes into identity theft and how to safeguard your credit information and other personal information from fraud and theft.

Chapter Eight, "Filing Bankruptcy," explains the Bankruptcy Abuse Prevention and Consumer Protection Act and how to determine whether you qualify for either Chapter 7 or Chapter 13 of the bankruptcy protection code. This chapter tells you how to file for bankruptcy protection and how to reestablish your credit after filing for bankruptcy. It also delves into debt management as an alternative to filing bankruptcy.

Chapter Nine, "Maintaining Good Credit," discusses the types of credit accounts and other consumer accounts that assist in maintaining good credit. This chapter includes detailed pros and cons of credit card debt, use, and costs. It also outlines those actions, credit accounts, and loans that will not help to maintain a healthy balance of credit.

CHAPTER

1

WHAT IS A CREDIT SCORE?

A credit score is a number generated by formulas known as mathematical algorithms. A credit score is established for about anyone who applies for credit, opens a bank account, or establishes bills in his or her name.

The algorithms make use of information contained in one's credit report and information supplied when one applies for credit. This information is used to create parameters that establish a credit profile and credit history for an individual. A statistical model is then used to compare these parameters to similar parameters gathered from millions of other consumers with similar credit profiles. Parameters that define one's bill-paying history, number of accounts, types of accounts, late payments, collection activity, outstanding debts, and age of accounts are processed with the algorithms to assign points to individuals. The total number of points assigned is one's credit score. To have a credit score, an individual must have at least one credit account that has been open for at least six months or have at least one report that has been updated within the past six months. The resulting score is a demonstrated likelihood of repaying debts, which is used by creditors as an assessment of an individual's credit risk.

A California-based company, known as Fair Isaac Corporation (FICO), developed the methodology used in generating credit scores. The methodology includes analyzing one's credit history and credit profile to generate a credit score. The FICO scoring model is proprietary and is generated by the three major credit-reporting agencies, but only licensed for sale by Equifax. The other credit reporting agencies may generate credit scores using the FICO scoring model and share those results with lenders and creditors, but these other agencies may not offer the scores for sale to their customers. FICO has adapted similar methodologies or modified the FICO scoring algorithms to develop other methodologies that are licensed for use and sale by the other credit reporting agencies.

The methodology used by FICO generates what is known as the FICO score, which has a range of 300 to 850 points. Most people score in the high end of the range, between 600 and 800 points. The national FICO credit score average, calculated by Experian, one the three major credit reporting agencies, is 676 points. The average FICO credit scores calculated for some major metropolitan areas, based on a sampling of two million credit profiles in 2004, are listed in Table 1 from highest to lowest average credit score. The metropolitan areas listed on the left side of the table have credit scores that fall at or above the national average, and the metropolitan areas listed on the right side of the table have scores that fall below the national average.

Metropolitan Area	Average Credit Score	Metropolitan Area	Average Credit Score
Minneapolis	707	Denver	675
Boston	705	Tampa	675
Washington, D.C	693	Detroit	675
Seattle	691	Miami	672
Cleveland	690	Orlando	671
Philadelphia	688	Atlanta	670
New York	688	Los Angeles	667
San Francisco	686	Phoenix	660
Chicago	680	Houston	655
Sacramento	676	Dallas	653

Table 1: Average Credit Scores

The higher one's FICO credit score, the less a credit risk an individual presents to creditors and lenders. A credit score of 720 points or higher is considered the most favorable for obtaining credit at the most attractive interest rates. Lower scoring is used as the basis for offering consumers higher interest rates or denying them credit.

Consumer credit scores are available to any legitimate business entity with a need to know. Lenders and creditors rely heavily upon such data to evaluate an individual's credit worthiness and to determine the interest rate that should be applied to any acquired credit. Companies may also access one's credit score for the purpose of determining whether to grant an individual employment, a lease agreement, a rental agreement, or whether to engage an individual in other types of business and credit transactions. The major disadvantage to this type of credit scoring is that it relies on information that is likely to contain errors or mistakes. Creditors and court systems may submit information or it may be acquired from public records and debt collection agencies. Information that reflects past and current financial obligations is entered and stored in computer databases with validation limited to the accuracy and integrity of the individual entering the data. Mistakes and errors are commonplace with these methods of data entry, and the only real method of validating and verifying the information is for the particular individual to check the data against his or her financial obligations. Entries made to credit reports may stay in the credit report for as long as seven years, or ten years in the case of a bankruptcy. Positive entries represent an advantage to the consumer, but negative entries may negatively affect one's credit for years in the future.

THE FAIR CREDIT REPORTING ACT (FCRA)

Public records such as death records, criminal records, real estate records, court decisions, tax liens, and bankruptcies are compiled by various government entities as required by law. Such records are generally available to anyone who requests access to them. Information such as employment records and tax returns are not considered public records and are protected from public disclosure by law. Consumer reports, however, include a combination of information gathered from public and non-public records. As such, consumer reports are protected from public disclosure. The Fair Credit Reporting Act (FCRA) was established as federal law to regulate how credit-reporting agencies use consumer reports and to restrict access to sensitive information contained in such reports. This act was created in 1970 and amended in the late 1990s and in 2003. Full details of the legislation are too complex to document here, but there are several key factors of importance that will be explained.

The FCRA differentiates credit reports from consumer reports and it also differentiates consumer credit files from consumer credit reports. A credit report is only a subcategory of the various consumer reports that are complied and distributed by national consumer reporting agencies. Likewise, credit-reporting agencies which compile and distribute credit reports, are a subcategory of consumer reporting agencies. Credit reports are the most widely known form of consumer reports, but other specialty reports are maintained by various consumer-reporting agencies. A credit report differs from a credit file. A credit file contains all of the information that credit reporting agencies collect on an individual. A credit report is a type of consumer report that contains a collection of information taken from the credit file and provided to creditors and other business entities that have a valid permissible purpose.

Under the FCRA, credit-reporting agencies have an obligation to do the following:

- Disclose an individual's credit file and credit score to him or her upon request. The disclosure provided by the FCRA is for a person's credit file, not the person's credit report. Credit reporting agencies must provide individuals with all credit information on file upon request, so long as the individual presents proper identification and pays any applicable fees.

- To investigate any dispute from consumers regarding entries made to their credit files and credit report. The FCRA requires that credit-reporting agencies investigate disputes initiated by consumers regarding the accuracy or relevance of entries in their credit files. Any entries found to be negative, derogatory, incorrect, or outdated must be corrected or removed from one's credit file.

- To limit access to credit information to those companies or legal entities with a valid permissible purpose.

Permissible purposes may include the following:

- Response to court order or a subpoena from a federal grand jury.

- Response to a legitimate company in connection with credit transactions of the consumer, employment, insurance underwriting, business transactions of the consumer, determination of eligibility for a license or other benefit granted by a government instrument based on an applicant's finances.

- Response to a licensing authority.

- Response to inquiries to determine if a consumer continues to meet requirements of an account.

- Response to the IRS.

- Response to requests by a head of state or local child support enforcement agency.

An employer or potential employer must acquire the written consent of the employee or potential employee before requesting credit information. Likewise, anyone without a permissible purpose must obtain written consent of an individual to access his or her credit report. Companies that receive a copy of one's credit report will have their request for the report listed in the "Inquiries" section of the credit report.

THE FAIR AND ACCURATE CREDIT TRANSACTION ACT (FACT ACT)

The FACT Act evolved as part of an amendment to the FCRA. The FACT Act was established in 2003 and phased in during

2005. It extends the scope of the FCRA by specifically addressing consumer reports that involve other than credit reporting. The U.S. Congress has designated companies that compile and disseminate these types of consumer reports as specialty consumer reporting agencies which report information on special areas of interest such as checking accounts, gambling activities, insurance, employment, rental information, mortgage financing, and medical transactions. The FACT Act defines standards for accuracy, privacy, limitations, and rights with respect to all types of consumer reporting. When lenders and businesses fail to comply with laws established by the FACT Act, they may be sued for damages in state or federal courts. Consumers have been awarded millions of dollars in such legal suits.

RIGHTS

The FACT Act is the specific component of the FCRA that provides consumers with the right once every 12 months to free copies of credit files maintained on them by the major credit reporting agencies. It also provides consumers with the right to free copies of consumer reports maintained by specialty consumer reporting agencies once every 12 months. The act further entitles consumers to additional free copies of their credit files if they believe they are victims of identity theft. If one's identity is stolen, the individual need only contact one of the three major credit-reporting agencies to report the theft and initiate a fraud alert. Previous laws required individuals to contact each individual credit-reporting agency.

The FACT Act provides active duty military personnel, who are deployed overseas, the right to place a special type of alert on their credit files, known as the active-duty alert. The alert stays in the military personnel's credit report for a minimum of one year. Any business entity that extends credit to military personnel with an active duty alert is required to contact such personnel at the telephone number specified for the alert or take other reasonable actions to ensure that any requests for credit are initiated by the particular military person or a family member authorized to do so.

The Soldiers and Sailors Civil Relief Act (SSCRA) of 2003 provides members of the military further rights as specified below:

- **The right to request that interest rates on pre-service loans and obligations be reduced to 6 percent**. The request must be made in writing with a copy of applicable military orders. Lenders must, upon receiving a compliant request, forgive any interest rate in excess of 6 percent. The SSCRA requires that lenders actually forgive excessive interest rates, not just defer them until a later date.

- **Special considerations regarding eviction due to a failure to pay rent**. The SSCRA provides that eviction cannot occur if the rent is less than or equal to $1,200 per month. Other special provisions apply to rents that are in excess of $1,200, but less than $2,400.

- **Special consideration for housing leases**. The SSCRA specifies that housing leases entered before the start of active duty may be terminated if military orders indicate a permanent change of duty station or a deployment for at least 90 days. The right to terminate a lease under these conditions is applicable even when the lease agreement fails to include a military termination clause.

- **The right to cancel automobile lease agreements**. The SSCRA specifies that automobile leases acquired for service persons or their family members may be cancelled if military orders specify a deployment of 180 or more days. Even if the automobile lease is entered while the service person is on active duty, the lease may be cancelled if orders specify a deployment of 180 or more days or if the deployment is for a location that is outside the continental United States.

- **The right to keep an established state of residence** for tax purposes when deployed out of state.

- **The right to request that court hearings be delayed by at least 90 days when military orders prevent a presence to defend oneself.** Judges may grant additional delays as warranted.

Members of the Reserve and National Guard are also protected by the SSCRA while they are on active duty. Protection begins with the date of entering active duty and usually terminates within 30 to 90 days of the date of discharge from active duty.

ACCURACY

The FACT Act also provides that consumers deal directly with creditors and other companies that furnish inaccurate information to consumer reporting agencies for entry on their consumer reports. The act makes consumer-reporting agencies, creditors, and other companies more forthcoming in sharing the information that they collect and disseminate about individuals. The act further provides that furnishers of inaccurate information must be responsible for investigating disputed information. As long as negative information is being investigated, furnishers may not continue to report the negative information without noting that the information is in dispute or, in the case of possible identity theft, furnishers may not report the negative information at all.

PRIVACY

The FACT Act gives lenders a new obligation to assist consumers in making sure that their information is correct, to provide assistance in safeguarding their identities, to assist in the early detection of identity theft problems, and to halt the dissemination of information when one's identity has been compromised. The act requires that financial institutions, lenders, and creditors establish procedures that attempt to detect acts of identity theft before the theft occurs. Many companies have complied, in part or in full, by incorporating software and programs that alert them to specific and suspicious activities. Such activities may include requests for a replacement credit or debit card, efforts to reactivate an unused account, or a change of address.

The act also provides for local police departments to assist in blocking fraudulent information from appearing on one's credit report. Consumers who suspect that they are victims of identity theft or other fraudulent activities are required to report the crime to their local police. There is no standard form or procedure established for this process. Each local department follows its own in-house procedures. However, consumers should expect to receive a police report that specifies the following information:

- Police report number.

- Date and time of the report.

- Police department and location.

- Name of the person who takes the report.

The police report serves as an indication that one truly believes he or she is being victimized by identity theft. It serves as evidence that a crime may have occurred when one has to deal with creditors, lenders, and other entities in an attempt to clear inaccurate account information from one's credit files. A police report also provides liability for victims in criminal prosecutions where the victim's name and personal data are the basis for the case.

LIMITS

The FACT Act requires that furnishers of consumer information notify consumers of any negative information reported to consumer-reporting agencies. Consumers must be notified either before the negative information is furnished or not more than 30 days after furnishing the negative information to a consumer-reporting agency. Negative information includes late payments, partial payments, missed payments, and all other forms of default. The act governs any business entity that extends credit to consumers as well as collection agencies that report to consumer reporting agencies. This type of early warning to consumers is expected to alert consumers to problems with an account and give the consumer an opportunity to stop any possible abuse in its early stages.

The FACT Act requires that creditors, insurers, and other entities who make use of information contained in credit files to generate mailing lists and send unsolicited offers of credit or insurance to provide a toll-free phone number for individuals to call to have their names removed from the list of persons to receive future offers. The toll-free phone number, 888-567-8688, may be used to remove oneself from the mailing lists of all national credit reporting agencies.

Prior to the FACT Act, credit card and debit card receipts visibly displayed the expiration date for consumer's credit cards and entire account number for a consumer's account. The FACT Act now requires that receipts from credit and debit card transactions show a truncation of account information. The act requires that only the last five digits of one's account number be displayed and that the expiration date be removed from receipts.

OBTAINING CREDIT FILES AND CREDIT REPORTS

The FACT Act amendment to the federal Fair Credit Reporting Act (FCRA) requires each of the three major credit reporting agencies to provide individuals with copies of their credit files, upon request, once every 12 months. The requirement specifies a free copy of one's credit file, not a free calculation of one's credit score. As of September 2005, credit files must be accessible to all U.S. citizens annually, regardless of their place of residence. With the exception of Georgia, consumers are entitled to one free copy of their credit file if they are unemployed and plan to apply for unemployment benefits within the next 60 days, receive public assistance, believe their credit file contains inaccurate entries resulting from an act of fraud, or if they have been denied credit, insurance, employment, or received some other adverse decision within the past 60 days because of a poor credit rating. Georgia residents are entitled to two free copies if their credit files per calendar year.

A central source has been established for the distribution of free consumer credit files. Free annual credit files may be obtained for one or all three of the national credit reporting agencies by making request from the nationwide central source using any of the following methods:

- Visiting the Central Source Web site at **www.annualcreditreport.com.**

- Making a toll-free call to
  1- 877-FACTACT (1-877-322-8228)

- Completing the Annual Credit File Request Form,
  which may be downloaded from the Central Source
  Web site, **http://www.ftc.gov/bcp/conline/include/**
  requestformfinal.pdf and mailing it to:

Annual Credit Report Request Service
P. O. Box 105281
Atlanta, GA 30348-5281

When consumers order their credit files, credit reporting agencies may also attempt to sell consumers a calculated credit score. Unless the credit reporting agency is Equifax, the credit score offered for sale will not be a FICO score. Instead the consumer will receive a proprietary credit score unique to the particular credit reporting agency. Only Equifax is licensed to sell FICO scores. In addition to the three major credit reporting agencies, other companies are licensed to sell credit files, credit reports, and credit scores based on information collected from the three major credit reporting agencies. Mortgage reporters are credit reporting agencies that collect information from two or more of the three major credit-reporting agencies to develop detailed or specialized credit reports for real estate lenders. The credit reporting industry also has resellers or brokers who act on behalf of several small creditors to purchase credit reports at a discount.

There are two types of credit reports — standard and investigative. Standard credit reports contain a complete outline of a consumer's financial history. The standard credit report includes personal information, tradelines, public record information, and inquiries. Investigative credit reports contain more detailed information about a person's lifestyle. Investigative reports are usually prepared when a thorough background investigation is needed, as with persons trying to acquire a multi-million dollar insurance policy or persons making application for a job that requires a security clearance.

Though consumers are entitled to copies of their credit files, the information compiled and sold to creditors, lenders, and other business entities is called a credit report. Credit reports contain information that is compiled from credit files, and a credit report is not likely to contain all of the information that is included in one's credit file. Companies may offer to provide consumers with free copies of their credit reports, but they may also require that individuals subscribe to a service or buy company products and services to get the free copy of the report. Consumers must read the fine print provided by these types of companies to be sure of exactly what is offered.

If individuals are not eligible to receive a free copy of their credit file, credit files may be purchased from the three major credit-reporting agencies by contacting them individually, as follows:

Credit Reporting Agency	Mailing Address	Phone Number	Web Address
Equifax	Equifax Information Services LLC P.O. Box 740241 Atlanta, GA 30374	800-685-1111	www.equifax.com
Experian	Experian P.O. Box 2002 Allen, TX 75013	888-397-3742	www.experian.com
TransUnion	TransUnion 2 Baldwin Place P.O. Box 2000 Chester, PA 19022	800-888-4213	www.transunion.com

Table 2: Major Credit Reporting Agencies Contact Information

The following chart shows fees required by each state per calendar year and the number of free copies of credit files provided to consumers within either one calendar year or a 12 month period.

State	Free Credit Files	Fee per Credit File
Georgia	2 per calendar year	$10
Colorado	1 per calendar year	$8
Massachusetts	1 per calendar year	$8
Maine	1 within 12 months	$5
Maryland	1 within 12 months	$5
New Jersey	1 within 12 months	$8
Vermont	1 within 12 months	$7.50
California		$8
Connecticut		$5 for the first report $7.50 for each additional file within 12 months
Minnesota		$3 for the first report $10 for each additional file within 12 months
Montana		$8.50
US Virgin Islands		$1
All Other States		$10
*Unemployed	1 within 12 months	
*Welfare	1 within 12 months	

Table 3: Credit File Fees by State

When making a request for a credit file by mail, consumers must include their full name, current address, social security number, any previous addresses that may assist with identification as well as a check made payable to the credit reporting agency, if applicable. A template that may be used to draft a written request for a credit file is shown in Form 1.

> * Residents of all states are entitled to a free credit report if they are unemployed or if they receive public assistance.

Form 1: Template for Letter Requesting Credit File

Credit Bureau Address   *05-23-2007*

To Whom It May Concern:

I was recently rejected for a *loan, job, or insurance policy* by *name of rejector* on *date of rejection*. The decision included use of a credit report from your service. I am requesting a copy of my report so I can review this matter. Please send my credit report to the following address:

full name (include middle initial and any jr. or sr.)
address
social security number
date of birth

Identity verifying documents are included with this letter. Thank you for your assistance..

Sincerely,
sign here

Credit reporting agencies collect, package, and sell financial information to lenders, employers, and other customers who have a need to purchase such information. These paying customers use the information to make decisions about lending money and offering other types of services.

The three major credit-reporting agencies support affiliate credit reporting agencies that collect credit information in specific regions of the country. The affiliates collect information and then pay to store that information with one of the chosen major credit reporting agencies. In return, the major credit reporting agencies pay affiliates to sell information to customers outside of the major credit reporting agencies' existing market. In fact, the credit reporting agency and the affiliate pay each other to sell information in each other's marketplace. Credit Data of New England, for example, is an affiliate of Experian. If a consumer lives in Credit Data's market area, that consumer is likely to be referred to Credit Data, not Experian, to resolve any issues with their credit file. If Credit Data should make a correction to the consumer's credit file, that correction will be automatically placed in the consumer's Experian credit file.

OBTAINING A CREDIT SCORE

The FCRA also entitles consumers to obtain credit scores calculated for them by credit reporting agencies. Unlike credit files, federal laws do not mandate that credit scores be provided by credit reporting agencies for free. If a consumer is in the process of obtaining a mortgage, he or she may be entitled to free credit score information as provided by the particular lending institution. Otherwise, the consumer is required to pay a fee to obtain a credit score.

Credit reporting agencies may provide consumers with credit scores, but the scores may not necessarily be FICO credit scores, which most lenders use. The three major consumer credit reporting agencies provide lenders with FICO scores, but the only credit reporting agency that has rights to market and sell FICO credit scores to consumers is Equifax. Consumers may also purchase FICO credit scores from **www.myFICO.com**.

When consumers purchase credit scores from the other two major credit reporting agencies, they receive a proprietary score unique to the particular agency. Fair Isaac Corporation develops these proprietary scores for use by the agencies, but the algorithms differ from those used to calculate a FICO score. Lenders who use TransUnion or Experian for their lending decisions are provided credit reports uniquely compiled by these reporting agencies, but the credit scores that they provide to lenders is a FICO credit score, not the same proprietary credit score they provide to consumers.

Along with a credit score, credit-reporting agencies provide consumers with up to four reasons for their credit scores. Reason statements are worded interpretations of reason codes that are provided to lenders. Credit reporting agencies have established more than 60 different codes that specify either or both positive and negative reasoning for one's credit score. As with the major credit scoring models, Fair Isaac Corporation is responsible for developing the most widely used reason codes and statements. Fair Isaac has developed reason codes and reason statements to complement the following specialty and classic credit agency scoring models:

Scoring Models	
NextGen	A broad-based next generation credit bureau risk score.
BEACON®	The scoring model used by Equifax.
EMPIRICA®	The scoring model used by TransUnion
Fair Isaac Risk Model	The scoring model used by Experian
Industry Option SM	Scores used by major credit reporting agencies in the bankcard, auto loan, installment loan, and personal finance loan industry

Fair Isaac Corporation holds copyrights to the complete listing of reason codes and reason statements that are provided to its customers (creditors) and prohibits the recording, retransmission, or other use of its listing for commercial gain. Fair Isaac does identify the reason statements shown in Table 4 as the most frequently used. The table also lists the associated classic credit bureau risk scores provided by Experian's Fair Isaac scoring model.

Reason Code	Reason Statement
01	Amount owed on accounts.
02	Level of delinquency on accounts.
05	Too many accounts with balances.
10	Proportion of balances to credit limits on revolving accounts is too high.
12	Time since delinquency is too recent or unknown.
14	Length of time accounts have been established.
18	Number of accounts with delinquency.
38	Serious delinquency and public record or collection filed.
39	Serious delinquency.
40	Derogatory public record or collection filed.

Table 4: Top 10 Reason Codes and Reason Statements

Reason statements also include tips to help increase one's credit score. Reason statements and their associated tips help consumers identify problems with their credit scores so that they are put in a position to correct those problems.

ONLINE ACCESS TO CREDIT FILES, CREDIT REPORTS, AND CREDIT SCORES

Credit reports may be accessed, downloaded, and printed online through a variety of resources if desired. Some companies also offer printed copies of credit reports for a fee. However, most states provide for consumers to receive a free copy of their credit file or a copy of their credit file at a reduced rate each year. Different credit reporting agencies offer variations in reported information. Most credit reporting agencies will attempt to sell credit scores in addition to credit files because there is no requirement for credit scores to be provided for free under the FCRA. Some variations of the information provided by online credit reporting agencies include the following:

- Credit files with or without a credit score.

- Three-in-one credit files that present entries from the three major credit-reporting agencies. These files may or may not include a credit score.

- Services that notify individuals when their credit history changes. This type of service may be requested on a daily or weekly basis.

- Subscriptions that allow individuals access to their credit file on a regular basis.

Online access to a credit file requires that an individual establish a user name and password to access the particular agency's database. In addition, the user will be required to answer a series of multiple-choice questions that are unique to the individual in an effort to verify their identity. Credit files acquired through TransUnion and Equifax are readily available for viewing for 30 days. Experian credit files are only available to a user for a single login session. Other companies may offer differing limits on access.

Consumers who are entitled to free copies of their credit files may gain immediate access to online credit files compiled by the three major credit reporting agencies from the central Web site at **www.annualcreditreport.com.** If a consumer is not entitled to the free copy of a credit file, the consumer may gain instant access at the respective Web sites of the credit reporting agencies. A service fee will be applied as indicated in Table 3. Credit scores are not provided at the central Web site but may be purchased from the individual credit reporting agencies or as part of some credit reporting services, three-in-one reports, or credit reporting subscriptions.

OBTAINING SPECIALTY CONSUMER FILES AND SPECIALTY CONSUMER REPORTS

Laws and regulations established by the FCRA and the FACT Act also govern specialty consumer reporting agencies which collect information about individuals in the same manner as credit reporting agencies from credit histories, public records, medical records, driving records, bankruptcy filings, and certain businesses with which an individual has a business relationship. This information is used to compile reports for companies in particular areas of interest, such as employers, casinos, or insurance companies. Unlike one's credit file, there is no centralized source for obtaining free specialty consumer files. Requests for consumer files must be made to the particular specialty consumer-reporting agency. Regulations do not require specialty consumer reporting agencies to establish a Web site or a method for mailing requests. Specialty consumer reporting agencies are only required to establish a toll-free phone number, which must be published everywhere that the agency does business. Specialty consumer reporting agencies are allowed to delay the processing of consumer's requests if there is a high volume of requests, as defined by the FTC. Agencies are required, however, to provide updates on the status of consumer requests. There is no required time limit for when this request must be processed. Though agencies are not required to establish an online presence, some consumer reporting agencies do have an online presence. Online agencies are required to provide a help screen or Frequently Asked Questions (FAQ) screen to assist consumers with their requests.

Consumers will find that one or two companies dominate the market for most specialty consumer files and reports. Other markets, particularly rental information and checking, have a number of companies that maintain consumer files. The consumer reporting agencies that provide specialty consumer reports for the various special areas of interest are shown in Table 5.

Special Area of Interest	Consumer Reporting Agency	Contact Information
Insurance	Choice Point (CLUE reports)	www.choicetrust.com (866) 312-8076
	ISO Insurance Services (A-Plus Reports)	www.iso.com/products/2500 prod2562.html (800) 627-3487
Medical	MIB –Medical Information Bureau	www.mib.com/html/request_your_record.html (866) 692-6901 TTY(866) 346-3642 for the hearing impaired
Rental Information	ChoicePoint (Tenant History Reports)	www.choicetrust.com (877) 448-5732
	Safe Rent	www.saferent.com, (888) 333-2413)
	UD Registry	www.udregistry.com (818) 785-3905
	Accufax	(800) 256-8898
	American Tenant Screen	(800) 888-1287

	National Tenant Network	(800) 228-0989
	Tenant Data Services	(800) 228-0989
	Tenant Screening Services	(800) 388-2335
Checking accounts	ChexSystems	**www.consumerdebit.com/consumerinfo/ us/en/chexsystems/report/index.htm** (800) 428-9623
	Certegy/Equifax	(800) 437-5120
	CheckCenter/ CrossCheck	(800) 843 0760
	SCAN Shared Check Authorization Network	**www.consumerdebit.com/consumer info/us/en/consumerreports/index.htm** (800) 262-7771 Fax: (800) 358-4506
	International Check Services	(800) 526-5380
	TeleCheck	**www.telecheck.com** (800) 835-3243
Employment	Choice Point (Employment History Reports)	**www.choicetrust.com** (866) 312-8075
Casinos	Central Credit Services	(702) 855-3000 (702) 262-5000
Mortgage Financing	Innovis	(800) 540-2505

Table 5: Specialty Consumer Reporting Agencies

NATIONAL CHECK REGISTRIES

There are three primary consumer reporting agencies responsible for maintaining histories of an individual's checking activities. They include SCAN, Check Systems, and TeleCheck. These, and the other consumer reporting agencies that are concerned with checking issues, are known as national check registries. National check registries only maintain checking information that banks report to them, and banks only report negative information. Check registries maintain a database of information that is available to members of the registry, retailers, and other types of subscribers. The information is used in making decisions regarding acceptance of checks or opening of checking accounts. The information is also used by database users to improve customer service, to assist in reducing losses from returned checks, and as a safeguard against fraud and identity theft. A sample report from the SCAN national check registry is provided in Table 6.

CONFIDENTIAL – for the use of: SCAN CONSUMER FILE DISCLOSURE REPORT	
John Doe 123 Penney Lane Seattle, WA 99999	SCAN Reference Number: 99999999

This report was prepared October 17, 1999 at 10:10 a.m. Pacific time. This information has been prepared by the Deposit Payment Protection Services, Inc. offices. Retailers and other businesses that subscribe to SCAN may require approximately two business days to update the SCAN database for any recent changes to your file.

Should you have questions regarding this information, please call 1-877-382-7226 or write to 12005 Ford Road, Suite 600, Dallas, TX 75234-72538 and refer to your SCAN Reference Number: 99999999

To Resolve individual items with a 'RETURNED' status, please contact the reporting Source/Payee. REPORTING SOURCE/PAYEE CONTACT INFORMATION can be found following the FILE INFORMATION section.

	IDENTIFICATION	

This report is based upon the following identification information you have provided to SCAN:

Bank/Financial Institution Account Number: 123456789   9999999
Driver's License/ID Number: WA   9999999XX9

THE FOLLOWING ARE BRIEF DEFINITIONS OF THE TERMS USED IN THE 'STATUS' COLUMN:

RETURNED: The check was reported to SCAN as returned to the payee unpaid by a financial institution.

ACCOUNT CLOSED: This account has been reported to SCAN as closed.

CLEARED: This item has been paid or otherwise resolved. For Account Closed items that have been cleared, the account has been changed to open.

	FILE INFORMATION				
This section contains check information furnished to SCAN by the Reporting Sources identified below.					
Driver's License/ID Number: WA 9999999XX9					
REPORTING SOURCE/PAYEE		CHECK DATE	CHECK#	CHECK AMT	STATUS
Big Stores	177	08/19/1999	322	$44.77	CLEARED 09/02/1999
Big Stores	163	08/19/1999	326	$12.01	CLEARED 09/02/1999
Small Store	12	09/12/1999	334	$240.01	RETURNED
Small Store	-- ACCOUNT CLOSED STATUS				
	REPORTING SOURCE/ PAYEE CONTACT INFORMATION				
Big Stores	(800) 555-5551 Store # 177 MON-FRI 8AM – 9:30PM, SAT 9:30-6PM CST				
Big Stores	(800) 555-5551 Store # 163 MON-FRI 8AM - 9:30PM, SAT 9:30-6PM CST				
Small Store	(800) 555-5599 Store # 12 Local Store Hours				
Please include this number in all correspondence: 42-99999999-9999999					

Table 6: SCAN Sample Consumer Report

The laws of the FCRA govern all national check registries. As such, consumers are entitled to a free copy of their credit file once every 12 months and may follow procedures established by the FCRA in disputing any inaccurate information. Unlike credit files that are maintained by the three major credit reporting agencies, consumer files that are maintained by national check registries are not immediately available online. Dependent upon the particular check registry, requests for consumer files must be made by phone, fax, or postal mail. The check registries that have a Web presence as listed in Table 5 provide the phone number and forms to be used in making requests on their sites. The ChexSystems and SCAN Web sites provide consumers with a sample of the file provided by their companies. Requests require that consumers provide personal identifying information, such as driver's license number, social security number, checking account number, and checking account routing number. If a retailer has declined one's check writing privileges, the request should also indicate the retailer's name, retailer's address, and date of declination. In return, a consumer file will be sent to the consumer via postal mail within five to fifteen days.

If after examining one's check registry report a consumer wants to dispute information contained in the report, consumers may make written requests to the check registry. A template that shows the form for a letter disputing information is shown in Form 2.

Today's Date

Check Registry Name
Check Registry Address
City, State Zip Code

To Customer Service

Ref: Check Registry Reference Number: 11-99999999-9999999

In reviewing the above referenced check registry report, I noticed that the following account information was included. Though the driver's license number reflects my driver's license number, I have never had a checking account identified by the account number given in the report.

Bank Account Number: 123456789   9999999

Driver's License Number: MD 999999999XX9

I have attached a copy of my check registry report and highlighted the information in question. I am requesting that this information be deleted and a corrected copy of my check registry report be sent to my address. Your prompt attention and response to this matter would be appreciated.

Sincerely,

Your Signature
Your Name
Your Address
City, State Zip Code
Encl: Check Registry Report

Form 2: Letter Disputing Check Registry Report

Gaming Credit Services

Global Cash Access, the parent company of Central Credit Services (CCS), owns the largest consumer reporting agency databases in the world for gaming patrons. This database is used to serve gaming industries around the world. The information contained in its database is used to profile gamers and determine their credit worthiness. Gamers are allowed to borrow money without the hassles associated with traditional lending methods. Interest-free lines of credit and other amenities are offered to gamers, regardless of their credit scores. Gamers need not pay the high interest rates for cash advances or the high ATM fees charged by the banking industry.

Gaming facilities are a part of a competitive market and various casinos must compete to retain patrons. It is estimated that 80 percent of a casino's profit comes from 20 percent of its patrons. Patrons who borrow the most money are rewarded with various amenities because the borrowed money is a potential profit for the casino if the gambler loses it. Some casinos have resorted to offering patrons pre-approved credit to lure a larger patron base. Casino gamblers need only access the casino's credit department to obtain a marker. A marker is a smart card with a unique ID number. The card is electronically linked to a file that contains the gambler's name, picture, birth date, social security number, and the gambler's casino rating. A casino rating is based on how much one bets, whether one wins or loses, and how long one plays. Casino ratings are kept daily and are cumulatively established over all previous trips to the casino. Facial recognition or some other form of biometric identification, such as fingerprint recognition or retinal eye scan recognition, is used to identity individuals who use the card. A marker entitles the gambler to interest free chips or cash with generous repayment provisions as well as customer service, special amenities, and a certain level of respect.

Casinos accumulate marker experiences and make them available to the CCS. If a gambler is late in paying off a marker, has too many markers, or has displayed questionable behavior, it is documented in the CCS database. The marker information is combined with information from consumer credit agencies and bank reporting agencies to create a patron profile that is stored in the CCS database. The CCS provides instant financial reports on casino patrons, who are referred to as whales by the casinos.

A line of credit may be established at casinos across the United States, including Native American casinos. Casino markers are available to all casino patrons, not just the high rollers. Application for a line of credit is typically required in advance of requesting markers. Application may be made by mail or via the casino's Web site. The amount of credit is based on the amount of money held in the applicant's checking account or other specified account. The casino will check the CCS file to determine whether a patron has outstanding accounts with other casinos that will hinder the patron's ability to pay any credit extended. Most casinos will extend lines of credit with repayment in 30 days with no interest or cash transaction fees. For most casinos, the actual period for repayment is dependent upon the denomination of money borrowed. Mohegan Sun, for example, is a casino located in Uncasville, Connecticut where the period for repayment is based on calendar days as follows:

Marker Denomination	Repayment Period (calendar days)
$1 to $1,000	7 days
$1,001 to $5,000	14 days
$5,001 and above	45 days

The casino allows patrons to consolidate individual markers to maximize the repayment period.

If patrons are not capable of repaying markers within 30 days or the established period for repayment, the casino may offer the patron some sort of assistance. Some casinos may extend the repayment period without interest, so long as the money was used for gambling and the marker was not acquired for purposes or activities outside of the casino. Casinos will not offer assistance to individuals who borrow money from the casino to pay outside debts and expenses, such as one's mortgage. The intent of lines of credit is for them to be used on the casino floor, not to pay bills. When patrons cash in casino chips, their CCS file may be accessed to ensure that the patron does not have any outstanding markers before cashing the chips, particularly when large chips are being cashed. Casinos are not likely to cash large amounts of chips if the gambler has outstanding debts for markers at any casino.

Lines of credit and markers provide security in casino transactions, eliminating the need to handle cash, checks, or ATM cards. They also relieve patrons from paying the high ATM fees that may range from $2 to $7 per transaction. The reality of markers is that when one acquires a marker, that person is effectively signing a counter check, which is a form of bank draft with the legal and financial obligation to repay the borrowed amount whether the patron wins or loses on the casino floor. Most casinos will allow patrons to indicate the preferred method of paying markers. Patrons may repay the marker directly to the casino or have the amount withdrawn from a checking account. Patrons may also return any unused markers to the casino, and in some instances; the casino may require patrons to redeem any outstanding markers as they win on the casino floor. Once all outstanding markers are redeemed, the patron's bank check is returned to the patron, eliminating the financial obligation of the draft.

New patrons may be required to settle any outstanding markers before they leave the casino. Seasoned patrons are allowed to engage in payment plans. In Atlantic City casinos, for example, patrons are required to sign a statement to establish a line of credit. The statement is an agreement that the patron will not leave with chips. The patron will not convert chips to cash while markers are outstanding, but will use those chips to redeem any outstanding markers.

Consumers may obtain a copy of their patron profile or dispute information that is contained in their profile file by contacting CCS directly using the phone number listed in Table 5 or contacting the headquarters as follows:

Central Credit Services
3525 East Post Road
Suite 120
Las Vegas, NV 89120

Medical Information Bureau

The Medical Information Bureau (MIB) is a nationwide consumer reporting agency that collects, maintains, and distributes records concerning information related to an individual's medical insurance, such as life, health, long-term care, and disability insurance. Generally, MIB files are held for individuals who have applied for one of these types of insurance products within the last seven years. MIB files are only established for individuals. No file is established for individuals who have applied for such insurance products as part of a group package.

Individuals with no significant medical condition and those who have not applied for insurance as an individual are not likely to have a file. MIB reports include information reported on insurance applications or information that insurance companies obtain from healthcare providers. Healthcare providers report medical conditions that insurance companies consider significant. The MIB has more than 200 codes to indicate significant medical conditions such as asthma, diabetes, high blood pressure, and depression.

Consumers may obtain a free copy of their credit report once a year by contacting the MIB using the phone numbers or Web address specified in Table 5. Consumers may also address written correspondence to the MIB as follows:

Medical Information Bureau
P.O. Box 105 Essex Station
Boston MA 02112

If after receiving a copy of their MIB report, consumers want to dispute information contained in the report, they may draft a letter similar to one shown in Form 2 to the MIB.

Rental Tenant Screening

There are a number of tenant screening companies that prepare reports for landlords on individuals who apply to rent housing. However, few of these companies are actually specialty consumer reporting agencies. As such, consumers are not entitled to free copies of the files established for them by these companies.

Companies indicated in Table 5 represent actual specialty consumer agencies. Consumers are advised to request potential landlords to provide contact information for the particular screening company chosen to perform its screening. If one of the companies listed in Table 5 is responsible for the screening, consumers may request a free copy of their tenant history report using the contact information provided in the table. If after receiving a copy of their report consumers want to dispute information contained in the report, they may draft a letter similar to one shown in Form 2 to the particular company.

Employment Screening

The FCRA outlines specific rules regarding background screenings performed by employers. The employer must provide employees and potential employees with notice that a background screening is going to be done before it is actually performed. The employee or potential employee must then provide the employer with permission to do so. Notice and permission for the screening must be a separate document from all other forms required as part of the job application.

A shortcoming of the FCRA is that the act does not require the employer to specify the company chosen to perform its screenings or to specify how to obtain a copy of the file compiled by the screening company. Employers need only provide such information if a potential employee is denied employment or a current employee is denied a promotion. However, California has enacted a civil code that requires employers to disclose the name of the screening company as part of the employer's notice and permission documents. California's civil code also allows employees and potential employees to obtain copies of the resulting reports generated by the company for two years.

The FCRA provides employees and potential employees with the right to a free employment file from established consumer reporting agencies that maintain files on employees and prospective employees. Hundreds of companies exist to provide employers with employment background screening, but they are not consumer reporting agencies. They offer to evaluate individuals and issue a one-time report to employers without maintaining files on individuals. The National Association of Professional Background Screeners has complied a listing of more than 300 such companies at **www.napbs.com.**

For individuals who seek employment outside California, their only recourse is to try to obtain disclosure of the company responsible for the screening and then determine how to get a report from the particular company. When employers use the services of ChoicePoint, the consumer reporting agency listed in Table 6, employees and potential employees may obtain their free file disclosure by contacting the company as indicated in the table. If after receiving a copy of their file consumers want to dispute information contained in the file, consumers may draft a letter similar to one shown in Form 2 to the Choice Point.

CHAPTER

THE CREDIT REPORT

A credit file is set up for anyone who establishes credit and engages in specific types of business and legal activities. Credit files are established for individual U.S. residents. Residents need not request to have such a file or apply to have a credit file. A credit file is established whether one wants one or not. Credit files are not established for joint parties or spouses. When a credit account is established for more than one party, such as accounts established with a cosigner or other authorized user, the credit history of the account is reflected in the individual credit files of all of the contractually binding individuals on the account.

Many credit reporting agencies, a specific type of consumer reporting agency in the United States, establish and maintain credit files. Some are specialty-reporting agencies that report data such as checking, gambling, and insurance activities. The three major credit-reporting agencies that collect and maintain individual credit files and then distribute credit reports on those individuals include Equifax, Experian, and TransUnion. Each of these agencies operates independently of the other two. Though the agencies provide similar information, they must compete with each other for business. As such, they provide different products, and they do not share information. Creditors may report account information to one agency and not the others. The information contained for any one individual may differ among the different agencies. When individuals request corrections and updates to their credit files, they must address each credit reporting agency separately.

Consumer reports are tools used by lenders, insurance companies, employers, and landlords to establish consumer profiles of individuals and to predict future behavior of such individuals. Consumer reporting agencies sell the collected information to credit grantors, employers, insurance companies, landlords, banks, casinos, and other legitimate business entities for a fee. Credit grantors use the tools to predict how likely an individual is to repay a loan, the interest rate to be applied to the loan, and what type of fees should be charged for the loan. Insurance companies use the tools to predict how likely an individual is to file a claim or have an accident. Employers use the tools to predict the trustworthiness of an individual. Landlords use the tools to predict whether an individual is likely to pay rent. Individuals may also use their own credit files as a tool to understand how their financial history is presented to creditors and other companies that access their credit reports.

One's credit file is crucial to the ability to acquire credit, and it is the responsibility of the individual to make sure that the information is accurate with each of the major credit reporting agencies before applying for any type of credit. Even though credit reporting agencies have a vested interest in maintaining an accurate system of reporting data, the credit reporting industry processes more than four billion pieces of data per month, and errors are inherent in this type of mass data processing.

WHAT IS CREDIT?

Credit is the ability to borrow money and the obligation to pay fees and interest on that borrowed money. Lenders or creditors issue credit to individuals based on information provided on one's credit report. Many private companies exist for the purpose of monitoring public records and creating and maintaining databases of consumers with and without public records. Creditors, primarily credit card companies, purchase databases of listings with consumers who have no public records. The existence of public records, or the lack thereof, is one of the standards that these creditors use in determining credit worthiness. These individuals are offered what is termed "pre-approved credit" with an application to be signed and completed. The fine print attached to the offer indicates that the issuance of credit is pending final approval and requests permission to examine one's credit report. What this really means is that the creditor is seeking permission to access the individual's credit report to determine if any other derogatory information is provided on the credit report since the individual has already passed the first test of having no public records. If no other derogatory information is found, the applicant receives final approval for credit in the amount offered. If other derogatory information is found, the applicant may receive final approval under the terms of the pre-approved offer, receive approval under different terms, or be denied the offer.

CREDIT IS DEBT

Credit is also responsible to create debt, which may be either secured or unsecured. Secured debt implies that an individual provides chattel that a creditor may repossess if the debt is not paid. Popular forms of secured debt are mortgages and vehicle loans. If a borrower defaults on mortgage payments, the lender may foreclose on the mortgaged property. Likewise, if a borrower defaults on a vehicle loan, the lender may repossess the vehicle.

Unsecured debt has no chattel to be repossessed. The most common form of unsecured debt is a credit card. Typically, the only security behind the issuance of a credit card is the borrower's willingness to pay any incurred debt. However, the credit industry also provides secured credit cards. The chattel behind a secured credit card is the funds put into a savings account for purpose of securing the credit card.

Debt provides a method of taking advantage of opportunities and experiences that enhance the quality of one's life and provide enjoyment and fulfillment. Homes, vehicles, vacations, education, and all of the things that enhance one's quality of life are obtainable by making good use of debt. Good use of debt requires that one develop a spending plan that incorporates methods of properly maintaining and managing the acquired debt.

Almost everyone will rely upon credit at some point. Whether credit is used to finance luxury and big ticket items, such as a car, or it is used to finance an unexpected medical or other emergency, one needs to be put in the position of being capable of acquiring the necessary financing when it is needed or wanted. By borrowing responsibly, one builds a positive credit history that indicates to lenders that they are a good risk for lending money. Most lenders examine one's past history of using credit in determining whether to issue additional credit. If one's credit history indicates a commitment to managing debt properly, the lender is more likely to extend the necessary financing when needed and also provide the most favorable interest rates and payment schedule.

With no debt and no credit history, an applicant represents an unknown risk, the same effect as having bad credit in the eyes of lenders and businesses.

Savings accounts established for securing a credit card earn interest like any other savings account, but the funds in the account may not be withdrawn from the account as long as it is used to secure the credit card. The account holder may make purchases up to the limit established by the amount of funds deposited in the secured account, or some issuers may allow purchases in excess of the amount in the account. The card may be used like any other credit card. The account history is reported to credit reporting agencies and only the issuer and account holder know that the credit card is secured. Secured credit cards offer two advantages: they allow the cardholder to rebuild credit, and the savings account continues to earn interest during the time for which the card is active.

PARTS OF A CREDIT REPORT

Credit reports are compiled for customers of credit reporting agencies using certain information that is contained in a consumer's credit file. The information is formatted into a credit report. Different credit reporting agencies use different formats, but each generally contains the same type of information. Though the section titles may differ, consumer credit reports contain the following general sections.

Personal Information

Entries of personal information are not used to evaluate one's credit history. These entries are collected from information provided on applications for credit and are used for cross-reference and identification purposes. Every time an individual applies for credit, the personal information supplied on the application is added to one's credit report. In other instances, information is mistakenly merged with data for another individual.

The personal information section of a credit report contains the following information for an individual:

- Name and any variations or extensions of that name, such as maiden names, Jr., Sr., or III

- Social security number.

- Birth date.

- Current and previous addresses.

- Current and past places of employment.

- Driver's license number and state of issuance.

Confusion over names is usually the reason for mis-merged data. When a parent and child have the same or similar names, their credit data may be mis-merged. Even individuals who have no relationship with one another but share the same or similar names have their credit data mis-merged. Individuals must be sure their credit file reflects their full name and that entries in their credit files are attributable to them.

An individual's current address should be listed first with any previous addresses held within the past seven years listed below. If one of the listed addresses is not a place where an individual has resided, the individual's data may be mis-merged with data for someone with a similar name. One's addresses provide a method for creditors to track an individual's place of residence and determine how long one has resided at a particular residence. When an individual moves too frequently, creditors may consider the movement as a sign of instability and an excuse to deny credit.

Account Summary

This section of the credit report summarizes all one's credit history. It includes a summary of all open accounts, closed accounts, credit limits, account balances, payment histories, and the number of credit inquiries. The account summary provides a condensed version of all information contained in the credit report, which may be many pages.

Public Records and Collection Accounts

Entries that are collected from court systems and from debt collection agencies usually have a negative impact on one's ability to establish or maintain credit. Not all credit files will contain this information, but most creditors will examine all available credit files when determining whether to issue credit. At least one credit file from the three major credit-reporting agencies is likely to have information obtained from public records or collection accounts. Credit reporting agencies make regular scans of public records to seek information to include in credit reports. Tax liens, judgments, bankruptcies, foreclosures, wage garnishments, and collection accounts are just some of the activities that become a matter of public record. As such, they appear in one's credit report for the time frames specified in Table 7.

TAX LIENS

Tax liens are placed against taxpayers' personal property by a taxing authority for the failure to pay required tax amounts. The

Internal Revenue Service (IRS) may assess penalties and interest against any outstanding tax debt that is owed. Further, the IRS may garnish wages and seize bank accounts without litigation in an effort to collect debts. If the debt is still not paid, the IRS will place a lien against personal property, and the lien information is included in the taxpayer's credit file.

If taxpayers cannot pay the debt, they should at least file their tax returns on time to avoid any additional penalties and interest assessed for the failure to file on time. They should also consider charging the outstanding tax debt to a credit card, borrowing the necessary money from a friend or relative, or requesting a repayment with the IRS. The IRS provides an application form that may be used to request a repayment plan. Taxpayers may also propose a payment plan with their filed tax returns. Any reasonable plan is likely to be approved, but the taxpayer must be sure to be capable of meeting the terms of any proposed plan. If a taxpayer is not capable of making reasonable payments on a tax debt or the outstanding debt is large, the taxpayer may propose an offer in compromise with the IRS. An offer in compromise is a settlement for a lesser amount than the amount that is outstanding.

Paid tax liens may remain in one's credit report for seven years or more years. These tax liens remain for seven years from the date they were entered by the court, not the date that they were paid. Unpaid tax liens remain in one's credit report until they are paid. Unpaid tax liens attach to personal property, such as a home, and may remain in an individual's credit report indefinitely. A tax lien against personal property attaches to the property as a second mortgage and it must be paid before the property is sold or transferred.

NON-TAX LIENS

Non-tax liens are assessed against personal property for reasons other than taxes. Non-tax liens may remain in one's credit file for as long as the lien remains filed against the consumer's property or until any applicable statute of limitation expires. Most major credit reporting agencies will remove tax liens after seven years, but there are many reasons that the lien may reappear in one's credit file. Equifax does not report property tax lien information.

JUDGMENTS

A judgment is a court decision about a lawsuit. A person being sued may be required to pay a judgment to the plaintiff in the suit if the plaintiff prevails. If the person being sued fails to respond to a summons to appear in court, the court may grant the plaintiff a default judgment. If a plaintiff believes that the facts of the case are straightforward, the plaintiff may request the judge to enter a summary judgment, which is a judgment issued without a trial. The court usually orders a judgment for the amount owed in addition to any applicable fees, such as attorney fees and court costs. Most states also allow interest to be applied to any judgment amount that is not paid immediately.

Creditors who are awarded judgments against consumers must follow rules established for the state in which the judgment is awarded. In some states, the consumer is required to disclose information about employment or personal finances to the court. Creditors may then use the information in efforts to collect the amount owed in the judgment. Creditors usually attempt to garnish wages, seize money held in bank accounts, or seize other liquid assets. When they cannot accomplish any of these acts, they will attempt to place liens against any personal property held by the consumer. If successful, a lien provides the creditor with the legal instrument necessary to take ownership of the debtor's property. Consumers should seek legal assistance from an attorney, or some form of legal advice for small claims if they are being sued by a creditor and believe they are not legally responsible to pay part or all of the money in question.

Judgments are acquired from public records. Judgments may remain in a credit file for up to seven years from the date in which the court entered them or the date established by the governing statute of limitation. The governing statute of limitation is the deadline for collecting a judgment as established by state or federal law. In some states this deadline may be 20 or more years. However, most major credit reporting agencies remove judgments after seven years even if they have not been paid. The party who is owed the judgment may then have a new judgment filed with the court if the judgment has not been paid. If an individual with an outstanding judgment buys a home, the judgment is automatically attached to the home as a second mortgage. If and when a judgment is paid, the credit file entry should reflect a paid a status.

BANKRUPTCIES

Bankruptcies filed under both Chapters 7 and 13 of the bankruptcy code are also acquired from public records and may remain in one's credit file for up to 10 years. Debts that are discharged in bankruptcy should be so indicated and not reported as charge offs. Like debts that have been paid, debts included in bankruptcy should be reported as closed. The appropriate chapter of bankruptcy should also be correctly reported. The three major credit reporting agencies and all Consumer Data Industry Association (CDIA) members have agreements to remove successfully discharged Chapter 13 bankruptcies from credit files after seven years from the date of filing bankruptcy. Each debt that is discharged under the Chapter 13 bankruptcy is also removed after the seven year period. If a Chapter 13 bankruptcy is not successfully discharged, the bankruptcy will remain in one's credit file for ten years.

FORECLOSURES

The terms of most mortgages conform to servicing guidelines established by investors or government agencies. Government agencies such as the Federal National Mortgage Association (Fannie Mae), the Federal Home Loan Mortgage (Freddie Mac), the Veterans Administration (VA,) or the Federal Housing Administration (FHA) establish guidelines for collecting delinquent mortgages. These guidelines generally provide the lender with options to assist the borrower in making good on mortgage payments such as accepting alternative payment arrangements. Other mortgages follow guidelines that are established by investor-owned mortgage pools. With mortgage pools, mortgages are packaged and sold in pools to investors. Lenders are less likely to assist the borrower with alternative payment arrangements for these types of mortgages. The guidelines established for these investor owned mortgages are designed to protect investors rather than the consumer.

For most mortgages, consumers are sent late notices when payments are late for one, two, or three months. When payments are delinquent for more than three months, the lender is likely to report the delinquency to credit reporting agencies and begin foreclosure proceedings. Foreclosure proceedings require expertise in real estate, and lenders would rather stick to the profession of lending. However, they are not going to ignore late payments. To avoid foreclosure, some lenders will offer financing options to assist the consumer. The availability of such options depends on whether the mortgage is owned by investors or a federal agency, whether the borrower's financial problems are long-term or temporary, and whether the borrower demonstrates a genuine interest in getting current. Some of the options that may be offered include the following:

HUD Assignment

A HUD assignment is an option available to FHA-insured mortgage holders who are suffering a financial crisis that is beyond their control. The assignment provides for HUD to become the mortgage lender and establish a workable payment plan for the borrower, provided there is a reasonable expectation that the borrower will be able to resume regular mortgage payments in 36 months.

Forbearance

Forbearance is an option offered by lenders to allow the borrower to make smaller monthly payments or suspend payments until the borrower's financial crisis has ended. Forbearance is generally granted for 12 months and, under certain circumstance, may be extended for 18 months. Forbearance is granted to borrowers who suffer temporary financial setbacks, such as unemployment or illness, which are not due to financial irresponsibility. The borrower must demonstrate good faith in trying to make payments.

Deed-in-Lieu

A deed-in-lieu is like a voluntary repossession where the

borrower assigns the property and deed back to the lender in lieu of foreclosure. By doing so, the borrower avoids having a foreclosure included in his or her credit file and the matter is ended. Some lenders, particularly those who are backing investor-owned mortgages, offer borrowers a small incentive to engage in this type of foreclosure avoidance option. However, these lenders are likely to exhaust all other avenues of relief before agreeing to a deed-in-lieu.

Loan Modification

A loan modification is an option that allows the lender to refinance the mortgage loan or modify the terms of payment to allow for more affordable monthly payments. The lender may also add the delinquent amount to the end of the loan as a balloon payment if the borrower demonstrates that he or she is able to make regular payments after the modification. A balloon payment is one large payment that is to be made at the end of the original terms of the mortgage.

Pre-foreclosure Sale

A pre-foreclosure is a sale of property by the borrower for fair market value of the property. This sale is only held with the permission of the lender who agrees to accept the proceeds from the sale as satisfaction for the default mortgage. Even if the proceeds are less than the amount owed on the mortgage, the lender accepts the lesser amount in satisfaction and avoids foreclosure.

Temporary Indulgence

A temporary indulgence is granted to borrowers on the condition that default payments will be brought current within three months. A temporary indulgence is granted only under unusual circumstances, such as when a new mortgage loan is pending the sale of the borrower's existing property.

Military Indulgence

Military indulgence is granted under the SSCRA, which provides that active duty military are protected from foreclosure under the following conditions:

- ❑ Protection is sought on a loan secured by a mortgage, trust deed, or other security in the nature of a mortgage on either real property or personal property.

- ❑ The property is still owned by the service member or a family member at the time protection is sought.

- ❑ The obligation originated before the service member entered active duty.

- ❑ The service member or a family member prior to entering active duty owned the property.

- ❑ The ability to make payments is affected by the active duty obligation.

If all efforts to work with the lender to prevent foreclosure fail, a foreclosure is inevitable. Foreclosures are not immediate; they may take several months to complete. Borrowers may try to sell the property within this time in an effort to prevent foreclosure. The borrower will need to make sure that the sale value is at least an amount necessary to pay the balance of the mortgage loan. If the sale amount is not enough to pay off the mortgage, the seller must make up the difference or the mortgage lender may sue for a deficiency judgment to cover the difference as well as foreclosure expenses. In selling property, sellers should steer away from quitclaim deeds, which may be offered by some buyers. Quitclaiming relinquishes the seller rights in the property, but it does not necessarily rid the seller of the loan obligation to the lender.

If the lender sells the foreclosed property and the sale amount is less than the balance of the mortgage, the lender may not find it cost effective to try to recover the difference. Instead, the lender may forgive the debt, and the borrower will be required to pay income taxes on the difference. The IRS considers a forgiveness of debt to be taxable to the debtor.

Foreclosures included in one's credit report before December 29, 1997 may remain in the credit report for seven years from the date of foreclosure. Foreclosures included after this date may remain for seven and a half years from the date of the missed payment that made cause for the foreclosure.

VEHICLE REPOSSESSIONS

In general, a lender may repossess a vehicle as soon as the borrower defaults on the contractually agreed upon payments. The exact definition of default varies from state to state. In many states, a lender may repossess a vehicle for default without giving notice of the intent to repossess. Other states require that the lender provide notice of the default and also provide the borrower with an opportunity to catch up on payments. The persons who physically repossess vehicles on behalf of the lender are known as "repo men." They may repossess a vehicle at any time of the day or night and they may enter onto the borrower's property to perform the repossession. However, they may not engage in a breach of the peace. Each state has laws that govern the definition of a breach of the peace. It may include such things as threats of violence, actual physical violence, removing the vehicle from a closed garage, or taking the vehicle when the borrower objects.

After repossession, a lender may either keep the vehicle as payment for the amount owed or sell the vehicle in an attempt to recover the loss. If the lender decides to sell the vehicle, the borrower must be notified of when and where the sale will be held so that the borrower is given an opportunity to participate in the sale. If the sale price of the vehicle is less than the amount still owed on the vehicle and the sale was held in a commercially reasonable manner, the lender may be able to get a deficiency judgment against the borrower for the difference. The sale must be held in a commercially reasonable manner. The lender may not just sell the vehicle at a bargain to a friend, associate, or family member and then expect the borrower to pay the difference. Some states prohibit deficiency judgments for repossessed vehicles.

Most lenders will allow the borrower to reclaim the vehicle by paying the entire balance of the loan as well as repossession costs. Some states allow a borrower to reinstate the vehicle by paying an amount that would make the loan current along with repossession costs. Repossession costs can be expensive and include such things as storage fees, a prepayment penalty, and the repo man's fee.

In most instances, a consumer may contact the lender when he or she is unable to make timely payments to negotiate a new payment schedule or refinance the vehicle. In some instances where the borrower consistently pays late and the lender accepts the payment without a complaint, the consumer may be protected from repossession on the grounds that the lender has effectively agreed to the newly established payment schedule. If a borrower can no longer afford to make payments, the borrower may arrange a voluntary repossession or sell the vehicle. A voluntary repossession occurs when the borrower voluntarily returns the vehicle and the keys to the lender. A voluntary repossession will not prevent the lender from demanding a deficiency balance, but it will eliminate the need to pay repossession costs. If the borrower sells the vehicle, the borrower uses the money from the sale to pay the balance of the vehicle and avoids repossession. However, if the vehicle is relatively new or the borrower initially financed the vehicle over many years, the borrower may be upside in the vehicle loan. Being upside down in the loan means that more is owed on the vehicle than it can be sold for. If a borrower is in this situation and cannot afford to take on the loss, the borrower may have to engage in a voluntary repossession. A risky alternative would be to sell the vehicle to one of the many companies that purchase vehicles that are upside down and lease them back to the seller as a method of lowering the payment required.

Voluntary and involuntary repossessions included in one's credit report before December 29, 1997 may remain in the credit report for seven years from the date of repossession. Repossessions included after this date may remain for seven and a half years from the date of the missed payment that made cause for the repossession. Should the lender be successful in obtaining a deficiency judgment for a loss on the sale of the vehicle, that court ordered judgment would also appear on the borrower's credit report for seven or more years.

WAGE ATTACHMENTS OR GARNISHMENTS

Wage garnishment is a court ordered process in which an employer is required to retain a certain amount of an employee's wages to pay a debt. A creditor or collection agency must receive a judgment from a court to garnish wages. The employee is usually given a deadline within which to pay the judgment in full or establish a payment plan for the judgment amount. If the employee refuses to make any type of payment arrangements or payment is not made as agreed, the collection agency or the creditors may obtain a Writ of Garnishment from the courts, which permits them to garnish wages. The judgment amount or an established payment amount is then garnished from the employee's wages before the employee is paid. Employees cannot be fired because of wage garnishment for a single debt. However, employers may fire employees if wages are garnished for more than one debt.

Federal laws establish that only a portion of an employee's disposable income may be garnished from their wages. Disposable income is the calculated income that remains after subtracting legally established deductions. Such deductions include the following:

- Federal, state and local income taxes.

- State unemployment taxes.

- Contributions to social security.

- State employee retirement deductions.

The portion of disposable income that may then be garnished is calculated as the minimum of 25 percent of an employee's weekly disposable income or the amount of weekly disposable income that exceeds 30 times the federal minimum hourly wage. If, for example, an employee's disposable income for one week is determined to be $300 then 25 percent of their weekly disposable income is calculated as follows:

$$.25 \times \$300 = \$75$$

Further, the federal minimum wage is $5.15, so that the amount of disposable income that exceeds 30 times the federal minimum hourly wage is calculated as follows:

$$30 \times \$5.15 = \$154.50$$
$$300 - \$154.50 = \$145.50$$

Since $75 is less than $145.50, the required wage garnishment amount is $75.

These limitations on wage garnishment do not apply to garnishments used to pay state or federal taxes. The limitations also do not apply when the bankruptcy court orders a larger amount of income be applied to wage garnishments to pay creditors under Chapter 13 bankruptcies, or a court orders additional garnishment to enforce a support agreement.

Laws that are more favorable to employees govern some states. Pennsylvania, South Carolina, and Texas prohibit wage garnishment, and Florida prohibits wage garnishment against the heads of households.

STUDENT LOANS

Delinquent student loans may remain in one's credit file for seven years. If the loan is brought current with at least 12 on-time payments, the lender may be required to remove the delinquency from the credit file. In some instances, delinquent student loans remain in one's credit report for more than seven years. When student loans are sold, consolidated, or placed in collections, the original date of delinquency becomes unclear. It is then the responsibility of the borrower to prove the original date of delinquency to have the negative entry removed from the credit file. There is no easy solution to resolving this problem.

ARREST, INDICTMENTS, AND CONVICTIONS

Records of arrest, indictment, or a conviction for a crime may remain in one's credit file for seven years from the date of release, disposition, or parole. This type of information is not generally provided in credit reports, but may be reported in other types of consumer reports, such as those provided to insurance companies and employers.

ACCOUNTS IN COLLECTION AND PROFIT-AND-LOSS ACCOUNTS

Debt collection issues are governed under the Fair Debt Collection Practices Act. Collection accounts and profit-and-loss accounts included in one's credit report before December 29, 1997 may remain in the credit report for seven and a half years from the date of original delinquency, not the date on which the debt was charged off or placed in collections. Accounts included before this date may remain for seven years from the date they were placed for collections. Some of these older accounts have remained in individual's credit files past the seven year limit. Traditionally, when collection accounts were transferred to a new collection agency, a new seven year period was started. As such, the original date of delinquency was lost in the shuffle. If the account holder is able to prove the original date of delinquency, credit reporting agencies are required to apply the seven and a half year rule. To prove the original date of delinquency, account holders should provide credit reporting agencies with either an old credit report showing the original account information, copies of account statements from the time of the original delinquency, or old collection notices associated with the account. Even if such documentation is not obtainable, the account holder may still dispute the outdated information in hopes of otherwise convincing the credit reporting agency to remove the information.

Current Financial Obligations and Account Histories

Financial institutions and other creditors report past and current financial obligations. This section of the credit report displays detailed information on all open and closed accounts held over the past seven or ten years. Unpaid accounts may remain in one's credit report for up to seven years from the date of last activity. An activity includes a payment or a charge off as uncollectible. Accounts that have been paid may remain in one's credit report for up to ten years from the date of last activity.

Accounts established for spouses during a marriage become the debt of both ex-spouses after divorce. Though a divorce decree may specify the ex-spouse to be the party responsible to pay a debt, the language of a divorce decree is not binding with creditors. If a designated ex-spouse fails to pay a debt as specified by a divorce decree, the other ex-spouse becomes responsible to the creditor, and negative entries may be correctly entered in the non-designated ex-spouse's credit report.

When one's insurance company, for whatever reason, fails to pay medical bills on behalf of the insured, the medical service provider may collect from the insured individual. When the individual fails to pay, the unpaid medical bills are placed in collections. The collection company is not going to seek payment from the insurance company but from the insured individual instead. Some creditors may ignore medical collection accounts if the account can be identified as a medical collection.

The various credit reporting agencies may use various terms, but each credit report will display the following parameters:

- Dates accounts were opened.

- Types of accounts (revolving, installment loan, mortgage, auto loan, bankcard).

- Account balances.

- Loan amount.

- Payment history for each account, including late payments.

- Credit limits.

- Unpaid child support and overdrawn checking accounts.

For the purpose of account payment histories, a late payment is 30 days past due if it is received at any time from 1 to 30 days past the due date. To clarify, if a creditor receives payment on the day after the due date, the payment, if entered in one's credit report, is reported as 30 days past due. A payment received between 30 and 60 days after the due date is reported to be 60 days past due.

Credit Inquiries

The credit inquiries section of a credit report indicates who has assessed one's credit report and when such access was requested. The entry indicates how long the inquiry will remain on the credit report. The types of inquiries that may be included in one's credit report include the following:

- **Inquiries made by creditors** for individuals seeking to establish new credit accounts or engage in other types of credit transactions.

- **Inquiries by an individual** for informational purposes.

- **Inquiries made for promotional mailings** by creditors within the past two years.

Too many credit inquiries by creditors for the purpose of establishing new credit over a short period of time are viewed negatively. An inquiry to engage in a credit transaction includes inquiries made by creditors when a bill has not been paid. When one fails to pay a bill, the issuing creditor may inquire into one's credit report to locate the individual and/or to determine if other creditors are being paid. If multiple inquiries from creditors result in a denial of credit, a newly inquiring creditor may have doubts about extending credit to the individual. Inquiries made by individuals for informational purposes and inquiries made by creditors for promotional purposes are not revealed to creditors or used in generating credit scores. As such, these inquiries have no effect on one's ability to obtain credit.

Optional Message

Individuals are allowed to add a message in their credit file that explains any extenuating circumstances regarding negative entries in the report. The optional message may be no longer than 100 words.

WHAT IS EXCLUDED FROM CREDIT REPORTS?

There are limitations on the type of information that may be included in credit reports. Credit reports may not contain the following information:

- Credit scores. Even though credit scores are derived from

information contained in a credit report, credit scores are not a part of the credit report. In many instances, credit scores must be purchased separately from credit reports.

- Gender.

- Race or ethnicity.

- National origin.

- Religious preference.

- Political affiliation.

- Checking and savings account information.

- Business account information. Business account information is excluded except when the individual is held personally responsible for a debt.

- Purchases paid with cash or paid by check.

- Personal lifestyle information. Personal lifestyle information includes friends and sexual preferences.

- Bankruptcies that are more than 10 years old.

- Charge offs that are more than seven years old.

- Collection debts that are more than seven years old.

Though limitations exist for the type of information that may be included in a credit report, indirect disclosures of personal information may be deduced or inferred from the information that is included. Personal lifestyle information, for example, is excluded from one's credit report. However, persons looking at an individual's credit report have been able to draw conclusions about an individual's lifestyle from their address history, employment history, the types of inquiries made, and the names of creditors included in the report. If a creditor is named as the Mental Health Center for Psychiatric Care, a person looking at the credit report may deduce that the individual is paying for some type of psychiatric care. The FACT Act has provisions that attempt to protect an individual's personal medical information. The FACT Act specifies that creditors may not obtain or use medical information in making credit decisions and consumer reporting agencies may not include the name, address, or phone number of medical creditors unless the information is coded so as not to identify the provider or the nature of the medical condition. Though bank account information is excluded from a credit report, if one defaults on a bank loan from the institution for which a savings or checking account is held, the default may be specified on the individual's credit report. Anyone viewing the credit report may deduce that a checking or savings accounts exists with the institution.

LIFE OF CREDIT REPORT ENTRIES

With a few exceptions, entries made in credit reports have a limited life and must be removed after a specified time. Except in California and New York, credit report entries have a life span of seven or ten years as specified in Table 7.

When a credit report is being prepared for a transaction involving a loan of $150,000 or more, employment with a salary of $75,000 or more, or a life insurance policy of $150,000 or more, the limitations specified in Table 7 do not apply. Under these circumstances, credit information may be reported indefinitely.

However, it is not usually included in credit reports but used for investigative purposes and included in other types of consumer reports.

Type of account	Life on Credit File
Credit Accounts in good standing	Up to 10 years from the date of last activity
Credit Accounts in bad standing	7 years from the date of last activity
Collection Activity	7 years from the date of last activity
Paid Collections—New York residents	5 years from the date of last activity
Judgments	7 years from the date filed (paid or not paid) or until the statute of limitation runs out, whichever is longest.
Satisfied Judgments – New York residents	5 years from the date filed
Paid Tax Liens	7 years from the date of last activity
Unpaid Tax Liens	Indefinitely
Paid or Released Tax Liens—California residents	7 years from the date of release or 10 years from the date filed
Unpaid or Unreleased Tax Liens—California residents	10 years from the date filed
Chapters 7 & 11 Bankruptcies	10 years from the date filed
Non-discharged or Dismissed Chapters 12 &13 Bankruptcies	10 years from the date filed
Discharged Chapters 12 & 13 Bankruptcies	7 years from the date filed
Consumer Initiated Inquiries for loans or other benefit—California residents	2 years
Employer Inquiries for positions with salaries greater than $75,000.	Indefinitely
Insurance Inquiries for more than $150,000 worth of credit or insurance.	Indefinitely
Criminal Convictions	Indefinitely

Table 7: Life of Credit Entries

PAYMENT NOTATIONS

Charge Offs

A charge off signifies that a creditor wrote off a debt or portion of the debt as uncollectible because of default. Most creditors must charge off delinquent accounts after 180 days of nonpayment, but some creditors have been known to do so sooner. The debt remains owed, but the creditor signifies that they were unable to recover the debt and places the delinquent account with collections. Both the creditor's charge off and the collection account will appear as entries in the delinquent individual's credit file. Charge offs are never a good thing to have in a credit report.

Paid-as-Agreed

Paid-as-agreed is one of the terms used to describe the good status of an account. Paid-as-agreed signifies that an account is current and being paid in a timely fashion as was agreed when the account was initially opened.

Closed

A closed account is an account that the individual or creditor terminated.

CHAPTER

CREDIT SCORING MODELS

A Credit Scoring Model is a complex set of calculations or algorithms, which are exercised based on a predetermined methodology that is used by creditors to calculate credit worthiness. Different creditors use different methodologies that include parameters that are dependent upon one another. Though various creditors use different methodologies, all algorithms include parameters that are defined by variables that may be obtained from a credit report. Such variables as credit history, timeliness of bill payments, outstanding debts, length of credit history, and new requests for credit are readily defined and available from credit reports. Algorithms also include other information that cannot be obtained from a credit report. Algorithms may include information such as occupation, length of employment, or home ownership, which is acquired from credit applications.

Consumers need to understand the methodology used by a particular creditor to be able to determine how various parameters affect each other and their credit scores. However, the methodology, parameters, and algorithms used by each credit reporting agency, including those used by the three major agencies, are kept secret. What is known is that some parameters have the effect of improving one's credit score while other parameters have the effect of reducing one's credit score. In any case, individuals with problem credit will find it difficult to improve their scores and it is likely to take some time to improve low credit scores. An increase in credit score takes place over time and requires an ongoing effort on behalf of the individual, not the creditors or the credit reporting agencies. Individuals must be diligent in paying down debts and successfully disputing any negative information contained in their credit report to increase their credit scores.

THE FICO SCORING MODEL

Most lenders use the FICO scoring model to determine credit worthiness and interest rates. Many other credit scoring model results are offered for sale by credit reporting companies to their customers, but lenders do not use them. Even the FICO scores provided to lenders by the three major reporting agencies vary between agencies. Most lenders have methods of averaging credit scores obtained from all three of the major credit reporting agencies to arrive at a final score.

Only Equifax credit reporting agency offers the FICO credit scoring model for sale to consumers. The other two major credit reporting agencies sell scores based on their own proprietary scoring models. Equifax, through a deal with myFICO.com, is allowed to sell credit scores based on the proprietary FICO scoring model. Experian uses their proprietary VantageScore scoring model. TransUnion uses its proprietary Personal Credit Score scoring model.

The FICO scoring model examines five key aspects of a credit report. They include the following:

- Payment history.

- Amounts owed.

- Length of credit history.

- Types of credit used.

- New credit.

The following percents show the approximate value that each of these aspects of a credit report adds to a FICO credit score calculation.

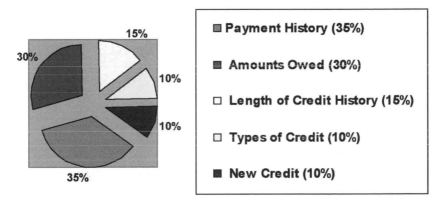

Payment History

It is good for consumers to have some sort of credit payment history. A credit report displays the payment history for all creditors from which credit was granted. Even after an account is closed and has been inactive, a credit report may indicate the history of payments over the period for which the account was active. However, having too many credit accounts and establishing certain types of credit may have a negative impact on one's credit score. Though open accounts may show a zero balance, the real interest for creditors is what the balance has the potential to be. An open account has the potential to be borrowed against and thus lowers one's perceived disposable income.

Payment history accounts for 35 percent of the FICO score calculation. It also represents the most significant aspect of the calculation. An individual's payment history includes information that indicates whether one pays the minimum balance due, more than the minimum balance due, or whether an individual pays an account in full each month. Payment history is determined by the following parameters:

- Number of accounts paid as scheduled.

- Negative public records or collection actions.

- Number of delinquent accounts.

- Total number of past due items.

- Length of time for which accounts have been past due.

- Length of time since the last past due payment.

Older individuals are likely to have long credit histories with lots of information in their credit files, while younger individuals are not likely to have many entries in their credit files. As such, a negative action, as the action relates to available information in a credit report, will have more of a negative impact on a younger person or any other person with a limited credit history.

Amounts Owed

A credit report displays the payment history for all creditors from which credit is granted. Creditors use this information to calculate the debt-to-credit ratio for individuals. Amounts owed include the following parameters:

How much is owed on accounts and the types of accounts with outstanding balances.

- How much is used of available revolving credit lines.

- Amounts outstanding on installment loan accounts and consistency in payments.

- Number of zero account balances.

Length of Credit History

The length of time that an individual has established credit will affect his or her credit score. Having no credit history or an insufficient credit history will have a negative impact on one's credit score. However, timely payments and low debt-to-credit limit ratios may offset the effect of an insufficient credit history. If one's credit history is less than three years old, opening too many accounts may signal a lack of credit responsibility. Length of credit history includes the following parameters:

- Total length of time tracked by the credit report.

- Length of time since accounts were opened.

- Length of time since the last activity.

Types of Credit

Almost all scoring models include an algorithm that measures the amount of debt acquired against the credit limit available. Further, the algorithm considers the type of credit acquired. Some types of credit accounts that may be included on a credit report are installment accounts, revolving accounts, and mortgages.

Some creditors consider some types of credit to be more risky than others. They are likely to consider the nature of the lending financial institution in assessing one's credit worthiness. Credit obtained from a finance company, for example, may be considered more risky than a mortgage loan, and have a negative effect on one's credit score even when payments are made on time. A mixture of account types is more likely to generate a better credit score than credit reports with numerous revolving accounts, such as credit cards. A mixture of installment loans with fixed payments, revolving lines of credit, and mortgages may improve one's credit score. Too many open and revolving lines of credit indicate being over extended and may have a negative effect on one's credit score since amounts up to the credit limit may become outstanding at any time. Too many installment loans may have a negative effect because the payment amount remains fixed until the debt is paid, limiting disposable income.

Some creditors may give more weight to credit accounts of the type they offer. A credit card company, for example, may give more weight to individuals who have a good history with other credit card accounts. Credit accounts should also include a mixture of secured and unsecured debts. An abundance of debt that is secured by personal property may improve one's credit score. In any case, the closer the amount of debt is to the credit limit, the more negative the effect on a credit score. Types of credit include the following parameters:

- Total number of accounts.

- Types of accounts.

New Requests for Credit

When a payee makes application for credit, the creditor will indicate such on the applicant's credit report as an inquiry. The number of such inquiries is examined and if too many new inquiries are reported, one's credit score may be negatively impacted. New inquiries are generally made within the past six months. New inquiries suggest that an individual is seeking to establish new credit accounts, and if all accounts are approved, the individual may be over extended. Inquiries may also be initiated and recorded when a creditor is monitoring an existing customer or pre-screening a prospective customer for a credit offer. Inquiries are only used in scoring model algorithms when an individual makes application for credit. In most instances where a creditor is responsible for the inquiry, it is not included in the credit scoring algorithms. Opening new accounts is encouraged for individuals who have past credit problems. However, these new accounts must show timely payments and must not max out the credit limit if they are to be an advantage. Most lenders will recognize multiple inquiries for a single credit line, such as inquiries for mortgage loans, if the inquiries are made within a short time. New requests for credit are measured by the following parameters:

- Number of accounts recently opened and the proportion of new accounts to the total number of accounts.

- Number of recent credit inquiries.

- Length of time since the most recent inquiries or newly opening credit accounts.

- Indications of re-establishing a positive credit history after encountering payment problems.

- Indications of attempts to open numerous new accounts.

FICO EXPANSION SCORING

FICO has developed a credit-scoring model for consumers who compose a relatively new market. The FICO expansion score uses non-traditional data acquired from credit agencies to develop a credit score for individuals who would otherwise not have a FICO credit score rating. The score is used to predict risk for consumers who do not have a credit history. The FICO expansion score is designed for young people who have not developed a credit history, recent widowers and divorcees who may not have credit in their own names, and new U.S. citizens and individuals who are diligent in paying by cash and have not developed a credit history. It is estimated that about 50 million citizens fall into the category of individuals with little or no credit history. The expansion score is intended to assist these individuals in conducting business that typically requires a credit check. The expansion score is expected to resolve the problem of having to pay higher interest rates because of a lack of credit history.

A lender is likely to pull an individual's credit report and credit scores from all three major credit reporting agencies and use the median or average score to process a credit application. When credit is being extended jointly to spouses, lenders may average the six credit scores obtained for the combination of both spouses. Some lenders may be willing to explain which credit scores they use and how those scores will affect a credit application, if such an explanation is requested.

THE VANTAGESCORE SCORING MODEL

VantageScore is a credit score model that was developed cooperatively by Experian and other national credit reporting companies in 2005. The VantageScore scoring model examines six key aspects of a credit report. They include the following:

- **Payment History.** One's repayment behavior is examined for all accounts to include an examination of whether payments are satisfactory, delinquent, or derogatory. Late payments have a negative effect on one's score

- **Use.** The percentage of available credit that an individual has used or owes on accounts. Using a large percentage of available credit limits indicates a risk.

- **Balances.** The amount of recently reported credit balances that have recently increased. This includes both current and delinquent credit balances.

- **Depth of Credit.** Length of credit history and the types of credit held. Long credit histories provide greater insight into how one manages credit and has a positive effect on one's credit score. A mix of credit types also has a positive effect on one's credit score.

- **Recent Credit.** Number of recently opened accounts and credit inquiries. Establishing new debt and applying for numerous accounts indicates a potential credit risk.

- **Available Credit.** Amount of available credit on all accounts. A low balance of available credit indicates good credit management and low risk. High balances, on the other hand, indicate potential overuse and may have a negative effect on one's credit score.

The following percents show the approximate value that each of these aspects of a credit report adds to the VantageScore credit score calculation.

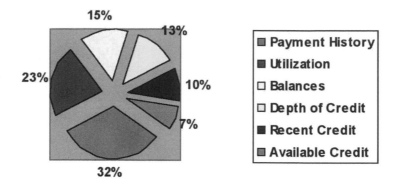

The VantageScore scale ranges from 501 to 990 points. The points of the scale are grouped and assigned an alphanumerical grade. Lenders may use the following grade system or use a different grouping to assign grades.

901 - 990: A   801 - 900: B   701 - 800: C   601 - 700: D   501 - 600: F

OTHER TYPES OF SCORING MODELS

In addition to the scoring models used by credit reporting agencies, creditors also use other predictive scoring models to calculate how likely consumers are to pay their debts on time in the future or how profitable an account may be in the future. These scoring models include behavior, profitability, bankruptcy, and insurance scoring.

Behavior Scoring

Credit reporting agencies use parameters from a consumer's record of payment on all credit accounts in their credit file for its scoring model. This type of scoring covers a broad range of credit activities. Behavior scoring makes use of parameters found in a lender's customer files. Behavior scoring is used to determine which customers are most likely to pay their bills on time. Parameters such as how many times one has been late on payments, how close one is to the credit limit, by how much one is late each month, how much of one's credit line is used to obtain cash advances, or how much one purchases on credit each month are obtained from a particular lender's files. These parameters are compared with those of other customers to determine how much of a risk a customer is. Behavior scoring is commonplace and used by more than half of all bankcard issuers. Lenders calculate behavior scores on a yearly or other basis to determine whether to increase credit limits. Behavior scores are also used in authorization. If, for example, one attempts to make a purchase that will exceed their credit limit, the authorization process initiated by the merchant is routed to the credit issuer. The credit card issuer then calculates a behavior score to determine whether to authorize the charge for the particular customer. Customers with high behavior scores are likely to be allowed to exceed their credit limit because the scoring model suggests that they exhibit good financial behavior. Customers with low behavior scores are likely to be denied the purchase.

Bankruptcy Scoring

Bankruptcy scoring is usually performed by credit reporting agencies and provided to lenders. Bankruptcy scores are based on parameters that may be found in one's credit file. These parameters are not directly related to paying on time, but are more concentrated on what type of job one holds, how long one has been employed at the particular job, how many accounts one has, how close one is to the credit limit, and how frequently one has moved. It is possible for one to make timely bill payments and still be characterized as a risk for bankruptcy.

Profitability Scoring

Creditors use profitability scoring to determine which accounts are most likely to generate the most revenue. The creditor also uses profitability scoring to target profit generating customers for incentives and special offers. Likewise, profitability scoring is used to weed out customers who are least likely to generate revenue. Customers who pay their bills on time, those who do not make many charges, and those who do not pay interest do not generate profits for the creditor.

Insurance Scoring

Insurance companies may use the FICO scoring model, but they have been known to tweak the algorithms to suit their own purposes. Their calculated credit scores are used along with other factors in determining whether to raise rates, underwrite policies, or deny insurance. Scores are also used in determining how likely one is to file a claim against the insurance company. This type of scoring is typical for auto insurers and a growing number of homeowner insurers. Insurance scoring is used for new applicants and for renewing customers. This type of scoring has raised concerns since it provides, for example, that drivers with a good driving record pay more for insurance if their credit history is poor. The insurance score is used to determine whether one is eligible for discounts on insurance premiums but may also be used to deny coverage. Some states prohibit insurance companies from denying coverage based on insurance scores.

CREDIT RISKS

Though credit scores in excess of 700 points fall into the norm of credit risks and are typically necessary to acquire more financing options and better interest rates, lower scores do not necessarily prevent an individual from obtaining credit financing. Lenders and creditors provide financing options to suit a variety of credit profiles. Credit scores among the U.S. population in 2003 averaged as follows:

Up to 499	1%		650 - 699	16%
500 - 549	5%		700 - 749	20%
550 - 599	7%		750 - 799	29%
600 - 649	11%		Over 800	11%

Consumers in the lower scoring ranges are considered higher credit risks and are forced to pay higher interest rates along with accompanying miscellaneous fees and charges. Though individuals may be classified as credit risks, there is no established norm for credit risks. FICO bases the norm on the range into which the largest percentage of individuals fall. Consumers who represent a normal credit risk fall in the scoring range of the largest percentage of borrowers. FICO considers consumers to represent a normal credit risk if the following apply:

- **Have a total of 11 credit accounts that are reported to credit reporting agencies.** Credit accounts include credit cards and installment accounts. They do not include savings and checking accounts. Of the 11 accounts, it is normal for a consumer to hold seven credit card accounts and four installment accounts.

- **Have never had a delinquency of 30 or more days reported.** It is estimated that 60 percent of consumers meet this criteria.

- **Have delinquencies of 30 days but not more than 60 days.** It is estimated that 20 percent of consumers meet this criteria.

- **Have a credit card balance of less than $1,000.** It is estimated that 50 percent of credit card holders meet this criteria.

- **Have an average of $12,190 in available credit lines** from all combined credit cards.

- **Have a credit card or a loan from the same source** for 13 years.

Most consumers fail to meet at least one of the criteria used to assess normalcy. The exact effect of meeting, exceeding, or failing to meet any one criterion is not clearly defined. However, some actions are known to have a negative effect on one's credit score. Missing one payment may reduce a good credit score by 50 to 100 points. Likewise, a bankruptcy may reduce a credit score by 200 or more points. Some financial institutions offer credit score simulators that may be used to determine how a specific action will affect one's credit score. Simulators specific to the FICO scoring model may be found at **www.bankrate.com** and **www.myfico.com**.

Some consumers represent higher than normal credit risks. FICO considers consumers to represent a higher than normal credit risk if the following apply:

- **Have a credit history** that is less than two years old. (5 percent of consumers)

- **Have an average** available credit limit in excess of $10,000 for all credit cards combined. (10 percent of consumers)

- **Had an account closed** by the lender or creditor due to default. (10 percent of consumers)

- **Have an account delinquency** of 90 or more days late. (15 percent of consumers)

Risk-Based Pricing

Lenders make use of credit scores in risk-based pricing, a method of predicting credit risks. Risk-based pricing methods are used to access risks in loaning money to persons with low credit scores. Lenders charge these consumers higher interest rates and fees. Loans are packaged and put into loan package groupings that are established by the range of interest rates that the lender is offering and an individual must have a certain credit score to fall within a certain loan package. The point groupings required for these loan packages depend highly on time and economic conditions. A sample of a loan packaging grouping is shown in Table 8.

Credit Score	Interest Rate
500 – 599	9.3%
560 – 619	8.5%
620 – 674	7.6%
675 – 699	6.5%
700 – 719	5.9%
720 – 850	5.8%

Table 8: Loan Package Groupings

CHAPTER

4

BUILDING CREDIT

If one's objective is to build a credit history, credit accounts need to be established so that payment histories are included in their individual credit reports. Timely payments are necessary to build or repair credit while unpaid bills may lead to collection activity and other negative entries on one's credit report.

CREDIT BUILDING ACCOUNTS

Consumers with no credit history or poor credit histories should choose to establish a checking account, savings account, or both. These consumers should also choose to establish an account history with a credit card company and be sure to make payments well in advance of the due date. The lack of a good credit history may require that they initially acquire credit with more high-risk types of creditors. As such, credit cards, charge cards, specialty credit cards, prepaid credit cards, secured credit cards, and other forms of installment credit should be sought. If a secured credit card is sought, a security deposit will be required.

Consumers with poor or no credit history should be aware of pre-approved offers that come in the mail. Creditors are allowed to pre-screen names acquired from credit reporting agencies and make pre-approved offers to those consumers who pass the screening. Once consumers accept the offer, a more complete screening that includes a check of their credit report may be performed and used as the basis to decline credit based on a poor credit history or to offer credit at a much higher interest rate than was advertised in the initial offer for credit.

Savings and Checking Accounts

Savings and checking accounts indicate to potential creditors that one has an established method for paying bills and a method of saving money. Savings and checking accounts are easy to establish and may even be established for minors with the use of joint accounts. Individuals may find it easier to establish a bank account by taking advantage of their employer's direct deposit program. Employer direct deposit programs allow an employee's paycheck to be deposited electronically and periodically into a checking or savings account.

Credit Cards

Credit cards are usually provided as a source of revolving credit. The creditor establishes a maximum credit limit and the consumer is allowed to make purchases against that limit. Credit cards allow consumers to carry forward a balance from month to month. As long as required monthly minimum payments are made on time and the balance is never allowed to exceed the established credit limit, the consumer will build credit. However, it is best if balances are kept well below the established limit when trying to build a credit history.

Charge Cards

Charge cards should be sought as an alternative to credit cards. Charge cards differ from credit cards because the balance of a charge card must be paid each month by making timely payments on charge cards. A consumer may quickly establish credit worthiness. Failure to pay the consumed monthly balance may lead to loss of privilege to make use of the card. Timely payments will eventually lead to offers for credit cards.

Specialty Credit Cards

Specialty credit cards include gas cards and retail cards, where purchases are limited to specific types of goods, usually those offered by the card issuer. Like other credit and charge cards, so long as monthly payments are paid on time and the balance is not allowed to exceed any established limit, the consumer builds favorable credit.

Secured Credit Cards

Secured credit cards are designed to help consumers with damaged credit rebuild their credit rating using a major credit card. These Visa and MasterCard credit cards allow consumers to make purchases up to the limit established by the savings account that secures the card. A savings account, CD, or money market account must be established to secure the card. If a savings account is used, a security deposit must be put into the account to secure the card. The money cannot be withdrawn from the account as long as the card is activated for use. Banks are willing to issue secured credit cards to customers with bad credit because the bank can collect from the security deposit if payment is not made. Some banks will issue secured credit cards to customers who have filed bankruptcy so long as the bankruptcy has been discharged. There is nothing on the card to indicate that it is a secured card and merchants who contact the bank for authorization will not be told that the card is secured.

The funds in the securing account earn interest during the card's activation period. However, some banks will not pay interest on the first $500 of a securing savings account, and the interest rate paid on amounts in excess of $500 may be less than that of a regular savings account. Finance charges will apply to the outstanding balance on a secured card and the rates are usually high. Interest rates may range from 18 percent to 24 percent. Secure credit cards may require an annual fee and an application or processing fee. These one-time fees are charged when the account is opened. Some card issuers will require that these fees be paid up front with cash, check, or money order. Other card issuers will include these fees with the first bill. Consumers should make sure that fees are refundable should they be denied a card. Other fees, such as late fees, bounced check fees, and over-the-limit fees are also assessed against the securing account when appropriate. Most secured credit cards offer a grace period within which the monthly balance can be paid without interest. The grace period is a benefit to cardholders who pay the account balance in full each month.

The competition in the banking market has caused some secured card issuers to offer cards at lower prices to encourage consumers to switch their savings accounts to banks that issue secured cards. This offer is usually reserved for consumers with good credit ratings, not those with bad credit. Nonetheless, the competition is lowering the cost of secured credit cards, and consumers are urged to shop around for the best deal. Some secured card issuers are offering interest rates on savings accounts that exceed those paid by other banks. In fact, some consumers are depositing their savings into these more profitable banks even when they do not need a secured credit card.

Customers need to make application for secured credit cards just as they would for unsecured credit cards. The bank will run a credit check and evaluate the application using more lenient standards that are used for unsecured credit cards. If the applicant meets the minimum standards required, they will be issued a card. Some cards are issued with limits established by the amount of funds deposited in the securing account. Other cards may be issued with limits in excess of the amount put into the account.

Secured credit cards may be used just as any other credit card would be used. Like any other credit card, cardholders are required to make monthly payments, and the account history will be included in the cardholder's credit file. When a cardholder misses payments on the account, the bank will not take the money from the securing account; instead, the bank will put the account through its collections process. Generally, the bank will not take money from the securing account unless the account is closed because the bank does not want to lose its paying customer. When the cardholder closes a secured credit card account, the cardholder will not be able to withdraw the funds from the secured account immediately. The bank usually puts a hold on the account for up to 90 days to allow any outstanding charges or credits to be applied to the account.

If the cardholder pays bills on time each month, for at least 18 months, some card issuers may convert the account to an unsecured credit card. Other card issuers may gradually increase the credit limit of the secured card so that the credit limit exceeds the amount held as security for the account. In some instances, it may take years of timely payments before an unsecured card is converted to a secured card. In other instances it may take months. In any case, an unsecured credit card will be attainable in the future.

Consumers must be aware of confidence artists who exist in the secure credit card market. Some con artists have set up post office boxes for applicants to mail applications and payment for secured credit cards. Some scammers collect the money and never issue a card. Other scammers forward the application to banks that issue secure credit cards, but with which they have no established relationship. The following tips will assist in determining whether an offer for a secured credit card is legitimate.

- **The name of the issuing bank should appear in the advertisement**. Visa and MasterCard require that marketers name the issuing bank in all advertising. If the advertisement does not specifically name an issuing bank, it is probably not legitimate.

- **If the offer guarantees a major credit card, the offer may not be legitimate.** Banks cannot guarantee approval. Some cards may be easier to acquire, and some banks may approve as many as 95 percent of the applications they receive, but there are factors, such as unpaid tax liens that banks consider to be cause for rejection.

- **If the security deposit is required to be held in a bank that is not federally insured, the offer may not be legitimate**. Federally insured accounts are protected for predetermined amounts should the bank fail or suffer some financial problems. Money held in uninsured accounts may be forfeited should the bank suffer financial difficulties.

A listing of legitimate secure credit card issuers may be obtained from CardTrack, Consumer Action, or **Myvesta.org**. Credit unions are also a good source of secured credit cards, though they may not offer a formal secured card program. Credit unions may be willing to assist their members in building their credit rating so that members are capable of purchasing more services from the credit union.

Prepaid Credit Cards

Prepaid credit cards are secured by the funds used to purchase them and they do not require a credit history. Prepaid credit cards will assist in building or improving a credit history. Individuals interested in building a credit history with this type of credit card will want to make sure to acquire prepaid credit cards from issuers who report credit activity to credit agencies. Prepaid cards allow for purchases up the amount that was prepaid for the card. Once the original prepaid amount is consumed, more funds may be reloaded to the card.

Installment Accounts

Installment accounts, such as those traditionally used to purchase vehicles and mortgages, are likely to assist in building one's credit so long as the terms of the contractual agreement are met. Installment accounts provide for an individual to borrow a specific sum and repay the amount along with the predetermined interest amount in regular installments over a fixed time. Vehicle loans are a common form of installment account used to build credit. However, individuals need to be aware of dealerships that offer second chance financing. Second chance financing is acquired through the dealership rather than traditional bank financing and may involve enormous interest rates and requirements to make additional purchases, such as extended warranties or life insurance. They are also more stringent and demanding than traditional lenders in their collection processes.

Major Purchases

Major purchases may increase one's credit score because such purchases are usually made with secured installment loans and the payment remains the same each month. The stability in making recurring payments from month to month is measured and assessed by creditors. Major purchases include home mortgage, vehicle, boat, furniture, appliances, a student loan, or other secured loans that are backed by the security of the item purchased.

UPSIDE DOWN LOANS

An upside down loan is secured by assets that are valued at an amount that is less than the loan amount. Many vehicle loans are upside down because a vehicle loses its value the minute it is driven off the dealer's lot. The problems with upside down loans come when trying to sell the securing asset. If one owes $21,000 on a vehicle valued at $25,000 and the vehicle is sold, totaled in an accident, or repossessed, the purchaser must pay the difference between what is owed on the vehicle and sale price or book value of the vehicle, whichever applies. In the case of selling a vehicle that is upside down in loans, if the sale price of the vehicle is less than any amount owed on the vehicle, the initial purchaser must satisfy the difference before the vehicle is sold. If the vehicle is totaled in a car accident and the vehicle is insured as is required by law, the insurance company is only required to pay the value of the vehicle as established by Kelly's Blue Book unless some form of optional insurance was acquired to cover the full value of the vehicle. If the vehicle is repossessed, it is sold at auction for the highest bid. If that bid fails to cover the amount owed on the vehicle, the initial purchaser from whom the vehicle was repossessed is required to pay the difference between the amount owed and the auction amount. In addition, the initial purchaser is required to pay repossession fees, attorney's fees, towing costs, and the auctioneer's commission. In many instances, the cost of repossession exceeds the original amount outstanding on the vehicle loan.

VEHICLE LOANS

The purchase of a vehicle usually requires some type of financing. Vehicle financing may range from a two to five year installment loan. One method of purchasing a vehicle is to use the equity one has in a home to purchase the vehicle. It offers tax advantages because the interest on home equity loans is tax deductible. However, the security behind the purchase of the vehicle is transferred to the home and if one defaults on the home equity loan, the home may be foreclosed on rather than the vehicle being repossessed. Another method of getting, not buying, a vehicle is to lease it. Leasing is much different than buying a vehicle because it is essentially the same as renting a vehicle, except that leasing may offer advantages over buying a vehicle. Vehicle leases usually require a small down payment and in some instances, no down payment. Vehicle leases are also tax deductible as a business expense for business owners. A vehicle lease agreement is a commitment to payments for an extended period of time that is reported to credit reporting agencies. This type of credit helps to improve a credit score.

Leasing a vehicle also has its disadvantages. Vehicle leases are costly and difficult to terminate. One cannot sell the lease or vehicle unless all of the payments are made. The terms of the lease must be satisfied in full before the lease can be terminated unless the leaser is a military service person ordered to active duty.

MORTGAGE LOANS

The purchase of a home usually requires mortgage financing. If one defaults on a mortgage, the lender will foreclose on the home and sell it to pay off the mortgage. The average cost for a lender to foreclose on real estate is about $25,000. The original homeowner would then be required to pay the difference between the amount owed and the sale price of the home. In addition, the original owner is responsible to pay the cost incurred by the lender to foreclose on the property. Home equity lines of credit and home equity loans are like mortgages because they are secured by the value of the home, but they are usually offered at lower interest rates.

Home Equity Loans Versus Home Equity Lines of Credit

A home equity loan is what used to be called a second mortgage. Money is borrowed in a lump sum to pay for a purchase. Installment payments are required monthly, at a set interest rate, for a set period of time. A home equity line of credit is a line credit with an established credit limit that is readily available to the borrower. The line of credit usually has a draw period, which is the time during which the borrower may access the line of credit, and the time at which the borrower must repay any amount withdrawn from the line of credit. The line of credit may be established as either an interest-only line of credit or the borrower may be required to pay interest and principal. In either case, any amount borrowed may be paid off anytime during the draw period without a prepayment penalty.

An interest-only loan allows one to pay only the interest incurred on the loan and the principal to be paid at a set time that is established by the loan agreement. Some lenders allow the borrower to determine the amount of the monthly payments. A borrower may, for instance, decide that they want to pay interest-only for one month and then principal and interest the next month

A home equity loan or home equity line of credit offers the benefit of adding additional types of borrowing to one's credit file. The borrower secures the amount borrowed by the same collateral that secures their mortgage loan, their home. Borrowers incur the same amount of debt that would have been incurred if they had opted for a larger mortgage loan. However, the debt is spread out among multiple types of loans that are included in credit files providing more positive information for the credit report. The disadvantage of acquiring additional debt against a home is that the borrower may become upside down in the loans, particularly if the value of the home decreases. If they ever need to sell the home, they will be responsible for paying the difference between the asking price of the home and amount of outstanding debt against the home before the home can be sold.

STUDENT LOANS

The U.S. government secures student loans issued to help pay the cost of higher education. Lenders receive a fee for originating and servicing student loans, but the government serves as collateral for the borrowed amount. When individuals default on a student loan obligation, they are subjected to the same collection procedures that are used for any other type of loan. In addition, the government may deny them access to additional student financial aid, confiscate any state and local income tax refunds, or garnish their wages. Further, schools may withhold transcripts of students in default of their student loans. Student loans cannot be deferred and they cannot be discharged in bankruptcy.

Student loans are reported to credit reporting agencies for inclusion in credit files. Student loans may be reported multiple times because they are usually applied for on a yearly or semester basis. For each enrollment in a student loan program, borrowers receive an entry in their credit file. As such, a student may have as many as four to eight student loans in their credit file. When the separate loans are paid on time, as agreed, the borrower's credit report benefits from having multiple credit accounts in good standing. This will improve one's credit score. On the other hand, if the loans become delinquent, the borrower has multiple credit accounts in poor standing that will reduce one's credit score.

After graduation, borrowers may consolidate multiple student loans into one loan. The advantage of consolidation is that borrowers may be able to get a lower interest on consolidation and extend the repayment period over a longer time. The original multiple loans are marked as paid in full in the borrower's credit file, helping to improve their credit score. Consolidated loans may also offer repayment options. The borrower may opt to make payments for the same amount each month until the loan amount is paid, they may opt to pay less in the beginning of the repayment period and then pay more in the later portion of the repayment period, or they opt to have a payment plan that allows the payment amount to change based on their income.

ACCOUNTS THAT WILL NOT HELP

While some types of credit accounts will assist in building one's credit, other account types may do nothing to help one's credit reputation. Some account types are not reported to credit reporting agencies. Other credit accounts are reported to credit reporting agencies but offer no benefit since they are not considered good credit references in the credit industry. Further, some of these unhelpful accounts require unnecessary fees and expenses and may cause the consumer unexpected problems if they are not used properly.

Passport Loans

A passport loan is against money that one has deposited into a bank account. A common method of rebuilding credit involves repaying the passport loan quickly and then requesting a larger loan amount. The problem with passport loans is that they may not be reported to credit reporting agencies and when they are, they do not provide as strong a credit reference as a secured credit card. If one chooses to use this method of building credit, they must be sure to choose a passport loan that will be reported to the credit reporting agencies and also ensure that payments are made on time. Some lenders allow for payments to be debited from the account holder's checking account.

Finance Company Accounts

Lenders have traditionally held loans from finance companies against consumers because the loans indicated that the individual could not qualify for any other type of loan. That perception has changed with the establishment of more legitimate and well-known finance companies. However, some lenders still look unfavorably upon certain finance companies, particularly those that claim to make loans to anyone. Consumers who are trying to build credit should avoid these types of loans since they are usually offered at the highest interest rates and they may not help in building one's credit rating.

One-Time References

Smaller companies that make a one-time report of credit accounts to credit reporting agencies or provide credit references to lenders will not do much to improve one's credit rating. First, most credit reporting agencies are not willing to devote the time and expense to check out these companies to see whether they are legitimate if the company is not a regular subscriber to the credit reporting agencies' services. Second, lenders base their loan decisions on payments made over time, and most lenders are not likely to contact such companies for a credit reference. Lenders pay for and rely on information that is included in credit reports.

Catalog Cards

Catalog cards are often referred to as paper cards, rather than plastic. They are only good for purchasing merchandise that is provided in the catalog provided by the card issuer. These types of cards usually require high fees to acquire the card and offer low quality, high priced merchandise. It is common for catalog cards to offer used electronics, cheap jewelry, or other defective merchandise. Catalog cards are often marketed under names that suggest that they represent major credit cards. They may advertise bogus gold cards or national credit cards. Some may promise that if cardholders pay accounts promptly they will be eligible for a Visa or MasterCard. Most catalog card issuers will simply pass the cardholder's application on to a secured credit card issuer. Consumers who make use of catalog cards are advised to request the name of the particular Visa or MasterCard issuer who will be issuing the credit card and then contact the issuer who will be working with the catalog card issuer. If the catalog card issuer refuses to provide the name of the credit card issuer, the catalog card issuer is likely to pass it on with no hope that it will be approved.

Rent-to-Owns

State usury laws do not govern rent-to-own accounts and they are rarely reported to credit reporting agencies. Rent-to-own accounts require that consumers pay an additional fee for rent and have that fee applied to a purchase at some later, predetermined date. These types of accounts are generally geared toward low-income consumers in hopes that they will default on the contractual agreement and forfeit the additional money that was to be applied to the purchase. Rent-to-own accounts may incur interest at as much as 200 percent and they do nothing to improve one's credit rating.

CO-SIGNING

A cosigner is a third party to a loan that guarantees repayment of the loan. A cosigner is responsible for paying the entire balance of a debt when the primary borrower defaults on payment. A borrower may be required to secure his or her debt with a cosigner if the borrower's income does not meet the income requirements of the lender, they have no credit history, or they have a credit history that does not meet the lender's criteria. The credit history of jointly held accounts is reflected on both the primary borrower and cosigner's credit report. When the terms of the contractual agreement are met, a co-signed loan may benefit both parties to the contract by improving their credit reputations.

Being a co-signer has some disadvantages. The primary borrower may have a tendency to rely upon the co-signer to pay the debt, and the primary borrower may not inform the co-signer of anticipated or existent delinquencies. When the primary borrower fails to make payments, the loan becomes delinquent and the co-signer is expected to make the payments. However, if the co-signer is not aware of the delinquency, it may take the creditor as many as 60 days to inform the co-signer that the primary borrower has defaulted on the loan payment. This 60 day delinquency may be reported in both the primary borrower and co-signer's credit file. In addition, the loan incurs late fees and other penalties. The co-signer will ultimately have to pay off the loan to restore his or her credit rating. While this should come as no surprise to the co-signer, it may end a relationship and create ill feelings between the two parties to the loan.

Before co-signing a loan, consumers are cautioned to establish a written agreement with the primary borrower so that the loan amount can be recovered if a default occurs. In such a case, the co-signer will not be relieved of any responsibility to honor the loan contract held with the creditor. The written agreement will only prove useful in a legal suit against the primary borrower to recover money spent to keep the loan current or pay off the loan. It might be best to co-sign only for small loans or short-term loans that may become less of a burden in the case of default. Further, when lenders examine a co-signer's credit report, the existence of the co-signed loan adds to the exiting debts of the co-signer, and the co-signer may be considered to have too much debt to qualify for an additional loan.

AUTHORIZED USE

Some creditors may allow for more than one user of an account. The primary account holder is given the option of authorizing someone else to make use of the account. The credit file of both the primary account holder and the third party to the contractual agreement will reflect the credit history of the account. To remove oneself as an authorized user of someone else's account, a person must make request to the issuer of the account.

Spouses or parents and their children most often practice

authorized use in an attempt to build one another's credit rating. A parent may add his or her child to a credit card as an authorized user and the account history is recorded in both parties' credit file. The parent receives the bill and makes timely payments on the account and both parties share the good account activity. If the child has bad or no credit history prior to the authorization, the good account information may help to build the child's credit rating and credit score. On the other hand, if the account becomes delinquent, the child's credit rating and credit score may decrease accordingly.

THIRD PARTY ACCOUNTS

Nine states are community property states in which a spouse is liable for the debts of the other spouse even when they are not aware of the spouse's debts. It only makes sense that the spouses co-sign or authorize use for each other in these states because they are already responsible for each other's debt. They have nothing to lose. If one spouse maintains a healthy credit rating, the other spouse benefits from the good credit history. If one spouse defaults on payments, he or she receives the benefit of the other spouse's good credit history being reported in his or her credit file to improve their credit score. The nine community property states are as follows:

Arizona	California	Idaho
Louisiana	Nevada	New Mexico
Texas	Washington	Wisconsin

EXPAND AND MANAGE CREDIT ACCOUNTS

Consumers with no credit history need to apply for credit and establish an initial credit account, usually with a credit card company. Special credit circumstances, such as marriage or divorce, may require specific strategies to get an application approved. Certain groups, such as college students, seniors, enlisted military, entrepreneurs, and immigrants may also require specific strategies for approval. Once a consumer with no credit history or poor credit history establishes an initial credit account, the consumer should seek to gain more favorable types of credit with lower interest rates.

Marriage and Credit

Before the Equal Credit Opportunity Act (ECOA) became law, creditors freely advised women to seek a husband or male relative to co-sign for credit. Creditors also asked details about women's childbearing plans and canceled women's individual credit accounts as soon as they married. The ECOA now establishes that women are entitled to credit in their own names if they qualify for it, or they may share a credit account with another person. Women cannot be requested to get a co-signer just because they are married or female. The only circumstances for which a lender may ask information about a spouse or other person are as follows:

- If the spouse or other person will also be using the account. The account is a joint account.

- The spouse or other person's income is being used to qualify for the loan.

- Alimony or child support is being used as income to qualify for the loan.

- The couple lives in a community property state.

- The couple is listing property that is located in a community property state.

When an account is shared, the payment history of the account must be reported in the credit file of all parties on the loan.

Creditors must give fair consideration to the income of both spouses in a marriage. When the source of income is alimony, child support, or public assistance, the creditor may consider the stability of such sources of income. If the party responsible for paying child support, for example, has a history of failing to pay, the creditor may reject a credit application for insufficient income. When a person is married, divorced, or widowed, creditors may not cancel their accounts if they continue to qualify for the loan. If joint accounts are held prior to a divorce or death of a spouse and the creditor has information, possibly from the initial application, that a spouse is not capable of handling the account individually, the creditor may request that spouse to reapply for a loan. The creditor may not freeze or cancel the existing account during this reapplication process.

Applicants do not have to disclose their marital status or gender on unsecured credit applications. Further, they need not indicate whether they prefer to be addressed as Ms., Miss, or Mrs. However, lenders may inquire as to whether one is married, unmarried, or separated when applying for secured credit. The lender is not supposed to use the information to discriminate. Lenders may also inquire about one's gender when applying for a home loan. The information is used for the purpose of government monitoring and if it is not revealed. The loan officer will be expected to assess gender information through observation.

Once married, a person's credit worthiness is evaluated differently. Creditors weigh a spouse's individual and joint debt against only the person's income when the person applies for credit alone. However, newly married couples should not share all credit accounts. If the marriage fails, it only requires one spouse to close all of the shared accounts, leaving the other spouse stranded with no source of credit. Also, the credit file of both spouses will be marked negatively for seven years if one spouse fails to make payments.

The ECOA allows individuals to have credit in their birth name, married name, or a combination of both. Individuals are allowed to keep credit accounts in their own name even when there is a change in marital status. To avoid any confusion, they should also use that name for legal and professional purposes. If a spouse decides to change her name after marriage, she is responsible for changing the name on credit accounts. Women are advised against using only the husband's name for credit. Jane Doe will have a credit history, but Mrs. John Doe will not. The latter only indicates that John Doe has a wife and there may be more than one of them.

Traditionally, men acquired credit accounts and requested that their wives be named as authorized users. As an authorized user, the wife was not required to sign a credit application so that she had no legal responsibility for the account. Even though the account may have been included in the wife's credit file, the entry indicated that she was an authorized user of the account, which means she was able to use the account but had no liability for the account. Depending on how a particular creditor evaluates credit worthiness, authorized use may not assist in building one's credit history. Women who are still in this situation should contact the creditor for such accounts and ask to make application as a joint applicant to the account. The account information will then be included in the wife's credit file as a jointly held account. After about six months of holding a joint account with a husband, the wife may then apply for credit in her own name. If she is rejected because of a lack of income, she may seek a secured credit account in her own name.

Divorce and Credit

When a marriage ends in divorce, any joint accounts remain the responsibility of both spouses. Even when a divorce decree specifies a particular spouse to pay specific joint debts, the other spouse has a responsibility to pay the debt should the assigned spouse fail to pay. The credit files of both spouses will reflect the delinquent account information. A divorce decree is a legally binding instrument between spouses. It has no bearing on the joint contractual agreement that the spouses shared with creditors. A divorce decree may only assist a spouse in recovering payments that were made on behalf of the other spouse when they failed to pay debts as specified by the divorce decree.

Joint accounts are signed by both spouses who agree to pay a debt. Authorized users are not considered joint owners and have no responsibility to the creditor to pay debts on accounts that he or she was authorized to use.

A spouse must be responsible to close all joint credit accounts when they divorce or separate. Otherwise, the other spouse may run up large bills and fail to pay them, leaving the remaining spouse responsible to pay the entire joint debt. Some creditors will allow for spouses to arrange new, individual lines of credit and transfer mutually agreed upon balances to the new accounts. If spouses are able to arrange this type of credit, they will maintain responsibility for existing debts and also protect themselves from any new charges. Other creditors require that the existing debt be paid in full before transferring an account to a single individual. If paying the balance in full is not possible, spouses should close the account from further charges. However, some creditors will not close an account without the permission of all parties who share the account. A spouse should then refuse to accept responsibility for any future charges and draft a letter to the creditor specifying a desire to close the account. The letter should be sent to the creditor via certified mail, return receipt requested. A copy of the letter should be sent to the compliance officer of the legal department of the credit issuer. A compliance officer is the person responsible for seeing that the creditor complies with federal credit laws. If the request is not honored, the spouse has good documented evidence that he or she made every effort to close the account and prevent any additional charges to the account in a legal dispute.

If an ex-spouse has already defaulted on a shared account that he or she agreed to pay, both ex-spouses' credit rating will be damaged. The non-default ex-spouse may choose to settle with the creditor to have his or her name removed from a delinquent account by offering to pay a smaller amount than the total balance. As alternatives, the non-default ex-spouse may sue the default ex-spouse for the money or be forced into bankruptcy. Under Chapter 7 bankruptcy laws, the non-filing ex-spouse becomes responsible to pay joint debts that are discharged in the bankruptcy because the spouse who files for bankruptcy is relieved of the debt. Under either Chapter 7 or Chapter 13 of the bankruptcy code, a shared credit account will be noted as "included in bankruptcy" in both spouses' credit files.

If a divorced ex-spouse has his or her credit rating damaged by the other ex-spouse's poor bill paying habits, the ECOA provides the damaged spouse with some relief in obtaining additional credit. If the reasons for credit rejection are accurate but do not accurately reflect the damaged spouse's credit worthiness, the ECOA provides that creditors must consider any evidence that the damaged ex-spouse presents to demonstrate individual credit worthiness. Most creditors will attempt to ignore this law unless it is brought to their attention. Evidence such as documentation that proves that the damaged ex-spouse paid bills on time and that the only negative marks in his or her credit file are those joint accounts that were shared with the other ex-spouse may sway some creditors. This evidence will not convince credit reporting agencies to remove negative marks from the damaged ex-spouse's credit file, but it may be used to convince lenders to extend credit, despite the negative mark, or convince the creditor who reports the information to the credit reporting agencies to drop it.

Widows and Credit

A widowed ex-spouse who does not live in a community property state should not have any liability for a deceased ex-spouse's debts, which were held in the name of the deceased only. However, creditors may try to collect from the estate of the deceased ex-spouse. Whether creditors really do try to collect depends upon several factors, including the size of the debt, the size of the estate, and how likely the creditor is to collect. Widowers should provide creditors who attempt to collect from estates with the contact information for the executor of the estate who is responsible to handle the matter.

A surviving spouse will have to continue to pay debts that were shared with a deceased ex-spouse. Creditors may request information from the surviving spouse so that they may make a determination as to whether the surviving spouse is able to handle the account or they may close any shared accounts. If shared accounts are closed, the surviving spouse still has an obligation to pay on the account until the account is paid. The balance of the account may be prorated by the probate court for the deceased ex-spouse's estate. If the surviving spouse is still not capable of paying the shared debts, he or she may need to seek professional assistance or file for bankruptcy.

Surviving spouses need to establish their own credit if they do not have credit in their own names. If necessary, they may seek to open a secured credit account.

The three major credit reporting agencies should be notified of the death of a spouse and be provided a death certificate as proof of the death. Surviving spouses may also submit the deceased spouse's information to 1-888-5OPT-OUT to prevent creditors from sending pre-screened credit offers to a deceased spouse and to remove the deceased spouse's name from direct mail and telemarketing lists.

College Students and Credit

Credit cards are consistently marketed to college students because creditors have a hard time finding new customers in today's market. College students present a market of customers who are more than willing to sign on for one or more credit card accounts. College students are not required to have an income or parental permission to qualify for a credit card. If they are of age, all they have to do is sign for the line of credit and a card is mailed to them. Creditors expect that college students will make use of their cards and continue as customers well beyond graduation. Despite a lack of income, creditors do not consider college students to be a risk because they anticipate that parents will pay their bills if and when they fall behind on payments. It may be a good idea for college students to get at least one credit card while still in school because the credit card industry is set up such that students will be rejected for credit once they graduate, unless they have a work history and an existing major credit card.

American Express targets college students and also offers them perks, such as discounts on airfare and merchandise. Students are usually required to pay a $55 annual fee to obtain a Green card. A Blue card requires smaller payments on the account and has no annual fee. Visa and MasterCard market to college students and require that they have some type of income. The income, however, may be as simple as an allowance, a savings account, or a part time job. Department stores and gasoline companies also market to students for their credit cards. Department stores usually charge high interest rates, which cause the account balance to grow quickly. It may take years to pay off if the student pays the minimum balance each month. Most department stores report account histories to credit reporting bureaus, but the cards do not present a strong reference to other creditors. Gasoline cards require that the entire balance be paid each month, though some offer revolving credit for certain repairs and tires. Gasoline card issuers do not regularly report credit histories to credit reporting agencies and may be of no use in establishing a credit history.

Seniors and Credit

Credit cards, if used wisely, may offer many benefits to seniors, even those who never adapted to the concept of borrowing and paying interest to credit card companies. Credit cards provide safety, convenience, and emergency buying power. Credit cards are safer for use than cash and even checks because they eliminate the need to expose such financial assets publicly when making purchases. They also eliminate the need to travel to and from the bank to make cash transactions. Credit cards offer convenience in mail orders, Internet, and telephone shopping. Most credit cards will provide assistance in disputing purchases. Seniors may notify the credit card issuer of the problem and refuse to pay the bill until the dispute is resolved. With cash and checks, seniors would be forced to deal with the merchant directly. Credit cards also provide convenience in travel because most hotel and car rentals require a major credit card to make reservations. Should seniors find themselves in an emergency situation, a credit card may be used to pay for the emergency, and the senior does not have to travel to the bank to withdraw cash before dealing with the situation.

Some seniors, however, have no credit history because they have always paid in cash. Retired seniors may own a home, have valuable stocks and bonds, or have a large savings account; however, their income may be limited. Most credit issuers will only accept applicants whose income meets a certain level. For seniors who are trying to establish credit, the ECOA provides the following rules to protect them:

- Creditors may not discriminate against Americans because they are over age 62.

- When creditors use age as a factor in their credit evaluations, anyone age 62 or older must be given a score that is at least as high as the best score available to someone under age 62.

- Creditors must include income from pensions, part-time employment, and annuities when evaluating credit applications.

- Creditors are prohibited from changing the terms of loans, closing accounts, or requiring their customers to reapply for credit simply because the customer reaches a certain age or retires.

- Creditors are prohibited from rejecting seniors for credit because their age makes them ineligible for life, health, disability, accident, or other credit related insurance.

These rules do not guarantee credit for persons who are age 62 or older. Creditors may consider the adequacy of collateral when a senior's life expectancy is shorter than the terms of a loan and whether the creditor's cost to acquire the collateral will exceed the available equity.

Enlisted Military and Credit

Persons enlisted in the U.S. military and their families may find it more difficult to obtain a credit card because their credit profiles differ from most other citizens. Military persons may have low incomes, exclusive of housing allowances, per diem, and other benefits. They also move frequently or live overseas. Military persons should be sure to include all of their income on credit applications. They should include housing allowances, per diem, and other benefits. They should indicate whether any of these amounts is tax-free.

Many overseas applicants are refused credit because their mailing address includes an Army Post Office (APO) box, which creditors associate with attempts to commit fraud. Creditors would rather risk denying credit to such individuals than extending credit to a potential fraud. Military persons stationed overseas should use a post office in their hometown or use the address of a trusted friend or relative for credit applications. By using the same address, these military persons get the added benefit of having a stable address during their credit history. The SSCRA also provides military persons with certain rights with regard to evictions, interest rates, foreclosures, and default judgments as discussed in Chapter One in the section," Rights," under the Fair and Accurate Credit Transaction Act.

Entrepreneurs and Credit

Some people who have their own business rely upon credit cards to provide easy access to cash without having to plead with a loan officer. Credit cards provide an effective method of record keeping for entrepreneurs and they also require relatively low interest rates. Other self-employed persons may find it difficult to acquire a credit card because creditors consider them risky. A study once showed that one in five people who filed bankruptcy were entrepreneurs. Self-employed entrepreneurs have the challenge of presenting their financial picture to creditors so that they look as normal and stable as the rest of the creditor's customers.

It is suggested that self-employed persons not name their business after themselves. A business that carries the owner's name signifies the owner. Entrepreneurs who establish their business such that they hire themselves and pay themselves a salary cause creditors to have to dig deeper to determine whether they are self-employed. Further, when these entrepreneurs have an employer who verifies employment information for the business, the entrepreneur will appear to creditors as a regular employee of a company.

Immigrants and Credit

The ECOA prohibits lenders from discriminating based on race or national origin; however, they may take into consideration whether an applicant is a permanent resident or immigrant when evaluating their credit worthiness. Creditors may reject applicants who are not citizens if it appears that it would be difficult to recover payment if the applicant were to leave the country. Though most applications for credit inquire as to whether the applicant is a U.S. citizen, some lenders do provide credit to non-citizens.

MANAGING DEBT

An individual who has established an initial credit account must be responsible to manage that debt properly. There are a number of ways to determine whether an individual has accumulated too much debt. Three of the most commonly used methods include calculating a debt-to-income ratio, calculating current ratios, and determining a comfort level.

Debt-to-Income Ratio Calculation

The debt-to-income ratio calculation involves comparing one's income with the amount spent to pay credit accounts. It does not include payments for utilities or taxes. Lenders use debt-to-income ratios in evaluating credit worthiness, calculated on either a monthly or annual basis. Monthly debt-to-income ratios provide a good look at one's day-to-day financial situation, but it may not account for long-term debt obligations that may threaten one's financial stability. Annual debt-to-credit ratios consider all of one's financial obligations.

To calculate a debt-to-income ratio, one needs to have the most current credit account statements to determine accurately the monthly payment amount and the current balance of all loans. For revolving accounts, which do not have a fixed monthly payment, the card issuer will be capable of providing instructions on how to calculate the monthly payment amount. As an alternative, the monthly payment amount on a revolving credit account may be estimated as 2.5 percent of the total amount owed on the account, i.e., multiply the balance of the account by .025.

As an example, a consumer has monthly debts for a mortgage, car, two credit cards, and a doctor's bill. The mortgage also requires that property taxes and homeowner's insurance be paid. The consumer's monthly debt is as follows:

MONTHLY DEBT		
Creditor	**Monthly Debt Payment**	**Total Debt Owed**
XYZ Mortgage	$1,000	$110,000
ABC Car Loan	300	8,400
MasterCard	35	890
Visa	25	640
EFG Surgeon	20	200
Property Tax	134	1,600
Homeowner's Insurance	50	600
Totals:	$1,564	$122,230

The consumer's income must also be determined. For the purposes of debt-to-credit ratio calculations, gross income is used. Gross income is the amount before taxes. Any additional steady income, such as income from child support, alimony, or investments must also be included. Income that is not guaranteed, such as bonuses, should not be included.

> ## AN ANNUAL INCOME IS CONVERTED TO MONTHLY INCOME BY DIVIDING THE ANNUAL INCOME BY 12.
>
> Monthly Income = Annual Income divided by 12
>
> Likewise a weekly income is multiplied by 52 to arrive at an annual income and then divided by 12 to arrive at a monthly income.
>
> Monthly Income = (Weekly Income x 52) ÷ 12

For our example, the consumer has only income from salaried employment as follows:

MONTHLY INCOME	
Type of Income	Amount of Income
Wages	$30,000 ÷ 12 = $2,500

The monthly debt-to-income ratio is calculated by dividing the total monthly debt payments by the total monthly income as follows:

Debt-to-income Ratio = Total Monthly Debt divided by Total Monthly Income = $ 1,564 ÷ $2,500 =0.625 percent.

The debt-to-income ratio is calculated as 0.625, but the ratio should be expressed as a percentage. To convert the decimal value into a percentage, multiply the decimal value by 100.

0.625 x 100 = 62.5 percent

The debt-to-income ratio is 65 percent, which is considered poor.

The higher one's debt-to-income ratio, the more risk that individual presents to lenders. A debt-to-income ratio of 36 percent or less is considered a healthy ratio that will qualify for credit, including a mortgage with little problems, provided the amount of income and credit history meet qualifications. A ratio between 37 percent and 42 percent is healthy for qualifying for credit cards, but may present some difficulties when applying for other types of credit. With a ratio in this range, consumers are more likely to qualify for VA and FHA mortgage loans, and some lenders will expect the consumer to pay high interest rates for those mortgages or reduce some of their debt. A ratio between 43 percent and 49 percent is considered high risk and signifies to creditors that an individual is close to having some financial difficulties, if they do not already. Consumers with calculated ratios that fall in this range should begin to take action to reduce the amount of debt. A ratio of 50 or more presents the highest risk to creditors. Consumers who fall into this range should reduce their debts before they get out of hand.

Most mortgage lenders use the 28/36 percent rule when evaluating debt-to-income ratios. The 28/36 percent rule specifies that to qualify for a mortgage, one's monthly house payment debt, which includes the mortgage payment, taxes, and insurance, should not exceed 28 percent of their monthly gross income. Further, the total of all monthly household debts, which includes housing and all other revolving and unsecured debts, may not exceed 36 percent of one's gross monthly income. Using the information from our previous example, the consumer's qualification for a mortgage under the 28/36 percent rule is as follows:

The consumer's monthly house payment debt includes the mortgage, property tax, and homeowner's insurance. The total house payment debt is $1,184.

CREDITOR	MONTHLY DEBT PAYMENT
XYZ Mortgage	$1,000
Property Tax	134
Homeowner's Insurance	50
Totals:	$1,184

The consumer's monthly gross income is $2,500, and $1,184 is more than 28 percent of this amount.

$$1,184 \div \$2,500 = 0.4736 = 47.36 \text{ percent}$$

The consumer's monthly house payment debt is more than 47 percent of his gross monthly income. This consumer will not qualify for a mortgage under a lender's 28/36 percent rule. Likewise, the consumer's total for all household expenses, calculated as monthly debt above, is $1,564, which is much more of a percentage of the consumer's income than required for the 36 percent portion of the 28/36 percent rule.

$$1,564 \div \$2,500 = 0.6256 = 62.56 \text{ percent}$$

The 36 percent limit allows for 28 percent of household expenses used for mortgage related debts and only 8 percent for non-mortgage debts. When mortgage lenders offer FHA loans, VA loans, and some first-time homeowner's program, they use more lenient rules with ratio limits as high as 41 percent. Consumers who are not capable of meeting these ratio limits are required to pay a higher down payment, get an unconventional mortgage loan, or pay down some of their debts before seeking a mortgage.

Current Ratio Calculations

The current ratio calculation is intended to correct the problem with debt-to-income ratio calculations. The problem with debt-to-credit ratios is that they include the low minimum payments that most credit card issuers require in the calculation of monthly debt payments. These minimum payments make it appear as though people can afford a credit card expense even though their total debt may be unmanageable and require years of payments before it is paid off. In contrast, the current ratio calculation is used to estimate a person's overall net worth. This ratio is also referred to as liability/asset ratio or a debt/equity ratio.

The current ratio calculation considers both liabilities and assets. Liabilities are the total that a person owes. The monthly debt calculation that was used in the debt-to-income ratio above provides a good estimate of a person's liabilities. Assets are what a person owns, such as savings, securities, real estate, pension benefits, automobiles, jewelry, furs, the cash value of life insurance policies, and artwork. The current ratio calculation requires a determination of the current market value of each asset held by a person. Insurance companies, the blue book, **eBay.com**, or the classifieds are sources that may assist in determining the market value of assets.

The current ratio is calculated by dividing total liabilities by the total of market values of all assets. The calculated value is then expressed as a percentage.

Current Ratio = Total Liabilities divided by Total Assets (expressed as a percentage)

A current ratio of 30 percent or less indicates healthy long-term debts. Consumers with this level of a current ratio should consider consulting with a financial planner or accountant to explore investment opportunities. A current ratio in the range of 31 percent to 50 percent is considered stable even though those with ratios closer to 50 percent are considered less stable. These individuals should consider paying down debts, particularly debts on depreciating assets. They are capable of managing their monthly expenses, but in the long-term, they are paying interest that could be spent better elsewhere. Consumers with a current ratio in the range of 51 percent to 75 percent should reduce the amount of unsecured debt with high interest rates and also make efforts to increase their assets. They should also establish an emergency savings account that is equal to three to six months of their household expenses. Consumers with a current ratio of 76 percent or more should seek the services of a financial counselor or other professional for assistance.

Determining a Comfort Level

The comfort level formula is not a quantitative formula but involves assessing oneself, identifying habits that lead to debt problems, and seeking assistance, or developing a strategy to change such habits and reducing debt. Some of the indicators of growing debt problems that need to be examined are as follows:

❑ Paying rent, making mortgage payments, or paying other bills late because one does not have enough money to pay them when they are due.

❑ Frequently making the minimum monthly payment on credit accounts.

❑ Credit card purchases are denied.

❑ Credit accounts with balances to the limit.

❑ Writing checks knowing they will bounce or in anticipation that an overdraft line of credit will cover them.

❑ Afraid that others will find out about debts.

❑ Using one credit card to pay another.

❑ Utilities are shut off or have been threatened to be shut off.

❑ Making charges with the expectation of paying them off soon and finding that there is not enough money to do so by the end of the month.

❑ Charging everyday expenses such as food and rent.

❑ Credit cards are cancelled due to tardy payments or charging over the limit.

❑ Receiving calls and collection notices from creditors.

❑ Ignoring billing statements.

❑ Charging purchases for others and requesting that they pay the amount in cash.

❑ Needing a co-signer for loans.

❑ Borrowing money from friends and relatives because one is denied credit.

❑ Using savings to pay bills.

❑ Lacking Insurance because one cannot afford to pay insurance premiums.

❑ Must work overtime or take a second job to pay debts.

Habits that result in ten of these indicators do not put one in any more financial trouble than someone whose habits result in one or two of the indicators. Each consumer is only required to examine why the indicators apply to them and whether it would be helpful to change their habits or seek professional assistance.

CHAPTER

5

REPAIRING BAD CREDIT

Bad credit is advertised to potential lenders and creditors by one's credit score. Bad credit has many consequences in the establishment of one's finances. It could cause consumers to pay more for borrowed money or cause a denial of credit. Furthermore, bad credit affects opportunities, creates stress, and puts consumers in the position of having to deal with creditors who take advantage of the lack of credit worthiness. Bad credit is acquired by failing to pay bills on time, carrying large balances with creditors, or being the victim of identity theft. Bad credit does not always equate to the failure to pay bills. Credit scoring models are used to calculate credit scores but are also used as predictors of credit risk in the near future. These predictions are based on an individual's borrowing patterns as opposed to their payment histories. A person may pay all of his or her bills on time, but their credit score advertises a risky pattern of borrowing that creditors may be concerned about.

Three of the five aspects of a credit report that are used in calculating the FICO credit score (discussed in Chapter Two:

Credit Scoring Models) have nothing to do with payment patterns, but are focused on borrowing patterns. These three aspects include the following, which compose 50 percent of a FICO credit score calculation:

- Amounts owed (30 percent).

- Types of credit used (10 percent).

- New credit (10 percent).

One's credit worthiness is determined in part by the amount and types of borrowing, the number of open accounts, and new applications for credit, as well as how close borrowed amounts are to available credit limits.

Identity theft is a relatively new and growing concern that has led to the destruction of credit ratings. With the advent of computers, electronic commerce, and online banking, vulnerable data storage and data transfer techniques have been compromised to the extent that personal information has been stolen and illegally used in financial transactions. Personal information may include account numbers, social security numbers, and other financial data that may be confiscated and used by computer hackers, company employees, and others with electronic access to the information. Electronic data processing has also led to the quick retrieval of personal information, which is then distributed in postal mail and other paper forms of communication. This information may be confiscated and used by friends, relatives, coworkers, and others with access to the information. Because of the growing problem with electronic theft, computer software manufacturers have established more secure methods of data storage and handling for e-mail, online banking, online purchasing and other electronic transactions.

Regardless of how one acquired bad credit and the resulting credit score, there are several things that one may do to improve a poor credit score and several resources that consumers may use to assist in improving their credit scores. At the same time, there are many unscrupulous companies that claim to be capable of improving one's credit score for a fee.

CONSEQUENCES OF BAD CREDIT

Creditors assess bad credit from low credit scores and bad credit offers several consequences to the consumer. In addition to higher interest rates for financing, consumers with bad credit are required to pay extra fees for financing. They may have trouble reserving hotel rooms, renting cars, or writing checks since most merchants require a credit card to complete these transactions. They may also be denied employment opportunities, be required to pay higher insurance premiums, or suffer marital problems, including divorce. Most consumers who suffer bad credit have had some type of financial difficulty that set them back. Financial difficulties may include periods of unemployment, serious illnesses, complicated divorces, new additions to the family, or businesses that fail. Unfortunately, the consequences of bad credit usually exist long after the financial problems are solved.

Higher Interest Rates

Interest rates are directly linked to one's credit score such that higher credit scores result in lower interest rates and lower credit scores result in higher interest rates. A difference of 100 points in credit scores may triple the interest rate required for a loan. Under the policy of universal default, all lenders with which a consumer holds an outstanding debt may raise the required interest rate if one lender raises the required interest rate due to a deteriorated credit score. Even when other lenders are being paid on time, lenders who operate under a universal default policy may raise interest rates to the penalty level.

Fees

Creditors and lenders may charge consumers additional fees in an effort to get consumers to focus on their particular obligation and to compensate the creditor for assuming the risk. Fees, such as over-the-limit fees, late fees, legal fees, repossession fees, penalties, default rates, and deficiency payments may be assessed against any amount borrowed. Fees may be assessed against both secured and unsecured types of credit. Consumers should take action when such fees are assessed. Some creditors may waive fees if the consumer makes an initial contact and offers a plan to get current with required payments.

Sub-Prime Loans

Consumers who present a high credit risk may be denied credit or be offered a sub-prime loan. A sub-prime loan is offered at an interest rate above the prime interest rate to consumers who fail to qualify for a loan at the prime interest rate. Consumers are encouraged to shop around for the best interest rate when their credit scores are not favorable.

Lost Employment Opportunities

Employers and potential employers may access an employee or potential employee's credit report. Credit report checks are a standard used in company hiring and promotion practices. Employees use the information as a method of assessing an individual's behavior in other aspects of his or her life. Employers may equate late payments with lateness for work or delinquencies with not being capable of following through on job duties. Research has indicated a correlation between bad credit and decreased productivity, and employers want to hire and retain productive employees.

Higher Insurance Premiums

Research has also indicated a correlation between bad credit and insurance claims. As such, insurance companies have used credit report information as the basis for increasing insurance premiums and denying insurance to consumers. Insurance companies reason that bad credit relates to financial stress, which may be distracting and may be cause for more accidents. The use of this type of practice by the insurance industry is being studied by the Fair Trade Commission and other interested parties. Some states have restricted the use of credit scores and credit reports in establishing insurance premiums. This issue is constantly evolving so that laws are subject to change and modification. The majority of states have some type of law governing the use of credit reports and scores in determining insurance rates, underwriting rates, and access to insurance. Fair Isaac Corporationoration, the developers of the FICO credit-scoring model, has also developed an insurance score which is calculated from data contained in credit reports. The methodology behind the algorithms used in calculating the insurance score differs from that used to calculate a credit score. Consumers are encouraged to consult with local state insurance departments for further guidance on whether insurance companies are allowed to make use of this or some other scoring model.

Increased Marital Problems and Divorce

Research has indicated that half of all marriages end in divorce and the biggest source of marital problems stems from financial issues. Bad credit is one of those financial issues that causes marital problems that may also lead to divorce.

MAKING APPLICATION FOR CREDIT

Creditors have no responsibility to extend credit to anyone who applies, but creditors are required to evaluate applications fairly without discrimination. After an individual makes application for credit, the Equal Credit Opportunity Act (ECOA) governs the application process and credit evaluations. This act requires lenders to disclose to applicants whether an application is accepted, rejected, or incomplete within 30 days of receiving all information necessary to process the application. However, consumers may not necessarily receive a response within 30 days because lenders are allowed additional time to acquire credit reports, verify employment, or receive other information. Credit card applications are generally evaluated within 90 seconds to one week, but the applicant may not receive a card in the mail for two weeks. If consumers do not receive a response to credit applications within 30 days, they should contact the issuing credit card company to find out why there has been no response. Consumers should have a copy of the submitted application to use for reference. Once a consumer has acquired one or more major credit cards, more offers for credit cards will be forthcoming.

The ECOA also prohibits discrimination against women and other minorities by creditors. The law prohibits discrimination based on race, color, natural origin, age, sex, or marital status. While the ECOA does not guarantee credit, it does guarantee that creditors will use the same criteria in evaluating credit applications made by women and minorities that is used for other applicants.

Credit Rejection

A rejection letter in response to a credit application is called an adverse action letter. The ECOA requires that lenders disclose to applicants, in writing, why an application has been rejected.

Some adverse action letters are easy to interpret while others may be confusing and offer few details as to what to do after being rejected. Two important pieces of information should be included in adverse action letters. They include the specific reason for rejection and the name and address of the credit bureau that supplied them with a credit report, if a credit report was used to make the decision. Though the ECOA requires that creditors disclose the specific reason for rejecting a credit application, the law does not specifically state that the disclosure be included in an adverse action letter. Creditors may provide contact information for the applicant to use to find out why the rejection occurred. Typical responses include providing the applicant with a toll-free number to call or providing an address to send a written request for the information. If an applicant receives an adverse action letter of rejection that does not disclose the specific reason for rejection, the law allows the applicant 60 days to contact the creditor to request such information.

The reason for rejection provided by a lender must be specific. A rejection letter may list one or more specific reasons for rejection, such as "credit report shows late payments in the past" or "insufficient number of revolving accounts." If the reason only mentions that information was obtained from a particular credit reporting agency, the reason is not considered specific. Applicants must be careful to scrutinize the adverse action letter of rejection for an adequate reason. The letter may disclose additional instructions that must be followed to get the required information.

Even when specific reasons for rejection are disclosed, the information may not help the applicant in determining exactly why the rejection took place. The ECOA only requires that creditors disclose the main reasons for rejection. Most creditors will only disclose two or three reasons for rejection when there may be many more reasons that are not disclosed. The ECOA does not require that the reasoning be provided in language that is reasonable for the consumer to understand. The law permits the language of reasoning to be disclosed in general terms. If length of residence, for example, is disclosed as the reasoning, the creditor is not obligated to disclose how the length of residence affects the acceptance or rejection of a credit application. Some creditors purposely provide reasoning that is vague so long as it falls within established legal guidelines in an effort to avoid lawsuits from consumers who may be wrongfully denied credit. Further, some credit scoring methods are so complicated that it is not always obvious why a particular applicant has been rejected.

An initial credit rejection is not final, but consumers must be diligent in finding out the reasons for rejection and requesting a copy of their credit file. Consumers should request a copy of their credit file from the major credit reporting agencies or, as a minimum, the credit reporting agency specified in the rejection letter that is responsible for providing the creditor with the credit file that was cause for the rejection, if such a credit reporting agency was indeed specified. If the request is made within 60 days of notification of the rejection, consumers may obtain a free copy of their credit file. It is possible that the credit file includes such inaccurate or incomplete information that the consumer may be able to correct it to qualify for credit.

Other Adverse Actions Against Credit Accounts

There are other situations when a creditor will take adverse actions against a customer's credit account. When a customer is refused an increase in their credit limit, a creditor closes an account, or a creditor makes other unfavorable changes, the creditor is required to disclose the reason for such actions.

If a customer is refused an increase in the credit limit of their account, the creditor must disclose the specific reason for the denial. If a credit report was the basis for the denial, the creditor must disclose the name of the credit reporting agency that provided the credit report so that the customer may request a free copy of his or her credit file. If a creditor closes the customer's account or makes other unfavorable changes to a customer's account, the creditor must disclose the reasons for the action within 30 days of changing or closing the account.

This rule does not apply when the creditor closes or changes the terms on most accounts that are similar. The rule also does not apply when the change is anticipated as with the expiration of an introductory rate or the inclusion of a penalty rate due to late payments.

If an applicant receives an offer of credit, but the offer does not include the same terms or the offer is not for the same amount advertised in the application, the applicant may refuse the offer. The creditor would then be responsible for providing the applicant with reasons that the offer was different than that applied for, within 90 days. If, on the other hand, the applicant accepts the modified offer and uses the associated card, the creditor has no responsibility to provide the applicant with reasons for the different offer.

CREDIT REPAIR

When individuals are experiencing problems with paying debts they may find themselves in situations which they may be capable of handling on their own or they may require the services of legitimate credit repair agencies. Individuals who are overwhelmed with debt, dealing with multiple financial problems, and in conflict over a suitable solution need to engage some sort of plan of credit repair.

Credit repair agencies have a history of scamming individuals with false promises of being capable of repairing their credit. Congress has enacted legislation that regulates the behavior of these companies by establishing strict guidelines regarding payment for such services and disclosures provided by such services. In general, credit repair companies are limited to performing the same types of activities that individuals are entitled to perform themselves, and they may not accept money in advance for their services.

The primary problems that consumers find themselves facing that are handled with the services of a credit repair agency include the following:

- **Multiple collection accounts.**

By using the techniques described below under "Steps to Repairing Bad Credit" one may be capable of handling a few collection accounts on his or her own. However, when individuals are faced with five or more collection agencies, they face various conflicting and unreasonable demands at one time.

- **Joint credit problems.**

Credit problems that are shared with another individual, particularly an individual who refuses to cooperate with problem resolution, may be best handled by making use of professional credit repair services.

- **Secured debts.**

Debts that are secured by collateral, such as mortgage loans, vehicle loans, and other loans backed by real or personal property could result in the loss or repossession of the securing collateral. Lenders of such loans tend to be less willing to work with consumers in resolving financial problems. In fact, the more collateral that secures a loan, the less willing the lender is to assist the consumer since the lender is put in a win-win situation. Some of these lenders purposely operate under rules that are complex and not well defined for the consumer.

Credit Repair Companies

Many companies claim to be capable of "repairing" a credit rating and credit score by recreating credit files with positive entries. Unless such companies are involved in some unscrupulous or illegal activity, such companies can do no more to improve one's credit than the individual can do alone. Legitimate credit repair companies may remove only inaccurate information from a credit report. They are not capable of removing information that is accurate.

The federal Credit Repair Organizations Act governs all credit repair companies. The act defines a credit repair company as any person or company that states either directly or indirectly that they can improve one's credit report. The act mandates that credit repair companies engage consumers in a contractual agreement, and it also mandates that they allow the consumer an opportunity to cancel the contract. The act further stipulates that a credit repair company may not make any statement that implies that they will alter one's identification to prevent the display of that person's true credit history. The act also prohibits credit repair companies from charging a fee in advance of performing their services. They are required to perform their services and then bill the consumer. Any such company that requests money in advance is in violation of the law.

The promise of many credit repair companies is to obtain a new credit identity for an individual. If the new identity involves a new social security number, it may be a scam and it may be illegal. Many of these companies are offering to provide individuals with a tax ID number or to form a fictitious corporation in the name of the individual. This may sound impressive, but these are things that one can do alone. Furthermore, these "solutions" may make the situation worse.

OBTAINING A TAX ID NUMBER

Any individual may form a business and apply to the (IRS) for a tax ID number for the business. The IRS requires that the applicant fill out a form and mail or fax the form back to them. In return, the IRS will issue the applicant a Tax ID number free of charge. A tax ID number is used to assess taxes on a business. Business transactions are performed using the business's tax ID number rather than the individual business owner's social security number. The problem with this solution is that any application for credit by the business will require that the business owner provide the creditor with his or her social security number.

Incorporating Oneself

The other option that credit repair companies offer is for individuals to incorporate themselves by forming a fictitious corporation. The corporation will need a tax ID number and the person being incorporated must pay any applicable fees for the establishment of the incorporation. The tax consequences of incorporation are such that the IRS taxes both the individual and the corporation. The IRS considers a corporation to be a legal person that is taxed separately from its corporate shareholders. As such, the IRS taxes incorporated individuals twice. As with any business, an incorporated individual will be required to sign for loans of the corporation, and creditors will require the social security number of the corporation owner. The time and expense of becoming incorporated is usually not worth it unless the individual really does run a business. In any case, creditors will require a social security number before issuing credit to a corporation.

STEPS TO REPAIRING CREDIT

Individuals who wish to improve their credit rating should engage in the following activities:

Stop or Reduce Credit Card Use

Consumers with poor credit should keep balances on credit cards and other revolving accounts low. The amount of money owed on outstanding debts accounts for 30 percent of a FICO credit score calculation. Credit card balances should be kept below 50 percent of the available limit. It is not good for consumers to owe large debts, particularly when the debt is spread out among many different creditors, reducing the consumer's debt-to-credit ratio that lenders and creditors examine in determining credit worthiness.

Opening new accounts in an effort to increase one's debt-to-credit ratio may have a negative effect. Opening new accounts may have the effect of causing additional inquiries in one's credit report. If many new inquiries are included in a short period of time, it could have a negative effect. Statistics indicate that six or more credit inquiries equate to an individual's being eight times more likely to file bankruptcy than if the credit report showed no inquiries. In addition, moving debts around from one creditor to another has the effect of maintaining the same debt with fewer open accounts. It may also provide a method of acquiring lower interest rates on the borrowed money. However, if those open accounts are maxed out, it could lower credit scores.

Consumers should keep open credit accounts to a minimum. When one's credit is poor, at least one credit card account should be maintained for emergency purposes. Also, it may be difficult to acquire credit in the future. If at least one account is left open, it will not be necessary to have to re-apply in the future.

Closing a credit account may not remove it from a credit report, but zero balances may have the effect of improving one's credit score so that unused accounts do not necessarily need to be closed unless the number of open accounts is excessive. A maximum of three revolving credit accounts is better than having ten open revolving accounts.

Consumers should also pay off home equity lines of credit. This type of credit is considered revolving credit, similar to that offered by credit cards since it allows individuals to borrow against securing property more than once. Paying down or paying off home equity lines of credit should have the effect of improving a credit score.

Find and Correct Credit Report Errors

It is estimated that up to 40 percent of all credit reports contain errors. Individuals must check that credit transactions are recorded accurately and that credit limits are reported accurately so that it does not appear that they have extended their limits. Individuals should also check for duplicate information in their credit files. If a mortgage has been sold to another firm, credit files should not falsely indicate a second mortgage. Other typical errors that may be included on one's credit report include the following.

OUTDATED LAST REPORTED PLACE OF EMPLOYMENT

Employment information is not regularly updated and usually reflects the place of employment when one initially files application for credit. Creditors do not usually update employment information when submitting updated credit information because employment information is not used in their decision making processes. If an individual has not applied for credit since changing jobs, the new place of employment is not likely to be included on his or her credit report. A credit report will not reflect a new place of employment unless a new application for credit specifies the new place of employment.

OUTDATED ACCOUNT BALANCES

Creditors make regular updates of credit histories contained in consumer credit files. Any reported account balance reflects the balance on the date on which the information is reported. If a creditor makes monthly updates to credit reporting agencies, payments or payoffs may not be reflected in one's credit report for a month after the payment or payoff was made. Balances with creditors who have longer update periods will take that much longer to be reflected in one's credit report.

DUPLICATE ACCOUNTS

Account data may be duplicated in one's credit report for several reasons. In some cases, creditors issue different types of credit accounts, such as revolving and installment accounts. The accounts may have similar account numbers, causing a single account to be entered as both an installment account and a revolving account. When an individual moves, a creditor may transfer his or her account to a different location and also give the person a different account number. As such, both accounts may be mistakenly entered on one's credit report. When a creditor charges off a delinquent account, the account may be placed for collections. When this happens, an entry for both the creditor and the collection agency will appear in one's credit report .In many cases, the collection agency will pass off the account to another collection agency. When this happens, only one collection agency entry should appear in one's credit report. The most recent collection agency account should be listed and the older collection account should be removed.

DISCHARGED DEBTS REPORTED AS CHARGE OFFS

In bankruptcy, when debts are discharged, the debt balance becomes zero and the credit report entry should indicate that the debt was discharged under the appropriate bankruptcy chapter. A charge off is debt that is not included in bankruptcy or a debt incurred after the bankruptcy. A charge off signifies that a debt is still due and owing. The creditor is satisfied that the debt will not be recovered and usually sells it to a collection agency.

OVERDRAFT PROTECTION ACCOUNTS

Lines of credit established as overdraft protection for accounts may exist in one's credit report even though the account for which the line of credit was to protect has been closed. These unused lines of credit should be closed, particularly for persons who already have available credit.

MIS-MERGED DATA

When information is mis-merged because an individual shares the same or similar name, address, or other personal information with another individual, all individuals involved are likely to find accounts on their credit reports that they never agreed to. Mistakes are often made in reporting social security numbers and names. Names with attached designations, such as Jr., Sr., and III, are easiest to confuse. The only way to remove such entries is to send written correspondence to the credit reporting agency that displays the incorrect data and the collection agency or creditor who is responsible for reporting the incorrect data. Documentation should include a copy of the credit report and detail each account that belongs to the individual and each account that belongs to someone else. The victim of the mistake must be careful to investigate the situation to ensure that the account was not stolen. Stolen accounts and identity theft are resolved in a different manner than mis-merged data.

DEBTS OF AN EX-SPOUSE

Debts resulting from any joint accounts held during a marriage become entries in both spouses' credit files. If the spouses divorce, the joint debts remain a part of both credit reports, even when they are assigned to a particular spouse as party of a divorce decree. A divorce decree, however, does not erase the original agreement made with creditors. If, on the other hand, and ex-spouse acquired debts individually, that debt should only be reported in the ex-spouse's credit file.

Identify the Errors and the Source of Errors

Entries on one's credit file are obtained from public records, creditors, and debt collectors. Debt collectors, also known as skip tracers, are hired to locate individuals and collect a debt. They use addresses provided in consumer's credit reports to contact current and past neighbors in an attempt to identify a delinquent consumers' place of work. They also contact listed creditors to seek an individual's phone number, address, work place, checking, and savings accounts. If one's credit file indicates errors, inaccurate references to late payments, or other negative issues that will lower credit scores, it may be possible to remove such negative entries without the assistance of companies that offer to repair credit reports and credit scores for a fee. The FCRA dictates that both the credit reporting agency and the furnishers of information have a responsibility to correct inaccurate or incomplete entries. Disputes may be settled by contacting the credit reporting agency or the creditor and collection agency whose reported entries are in dispute. Consumers may follow the form of the template shown in Form 3 to dispute information that is contained in their credit file.

April 7, 2007

Complaint Department
Name of Credit Agency
Address
City, State, Zip

To Whom It May Concern:

I am writing to dispute the following information in my credit report:
[Identify item(s) disputed by name of source, such as creditor or tax court, and identify type of item, such as credit account, judgement, and so on]

I have circled the items that I am disputing on the copy of my credit report attached to this letter.

This item is *[inacccurate or incomplete]* because *[describe what is inaccurate or incomplete and why]*. I am requesting that the item be deleted *[or request another specific change]* to correct the information.

I have enclosed copies of *[describe any enclosed documentation, such as payment records, court documents]*. These documents support my position. Please reinvestigate this matter and *[delete or correct]* the disputed item(s) as soon as possible.

Sincerely,

Name
Address
City, State, Zip

Enclosures: *[List what you are enclosing]*

Form 3: Template for Letter Disputing Credit File Information

CREDIT REPORTING AGENCY ERRORS

A letter of dispute should be sent to the credit reporting agency. Dispute resolution may also be initiated over the phone or online through links designed for such purpose on the credit reporting agency's Web site. A letter of dispute should also be sent directly to the creditor responsible for reporting the disputed information. Consumers should refer to the creditor's billing statements to find the correct contact information for disputes. The address is usually different from a creditor's payment address.

After errors have been identified, a consumer may request that the credit reporting agency investigate the disputed information and correct or delete it. Consumers may also request that credit reporting agencies delete outdated information. Credit reporting agencies have a responsibility to investigate disputed information upon request, unless the reporting agency considers the dispute to be frivolous. The reporting agency must notify consumers within five days of their decision to label the dispute as frivolous. They must indicate why the dispute was considered frivolous and explain what the consumer must do to make the dispute legitimate.

Though requests to investigate a dispute may be initiated by phone, written and online requests are recommended because they create a trail of documentation for future reference, if needed. Requests for investigation must explain each dispute clearly and request an investigation to resolve issues. A copy of the credit file and supporting documentation should be included in the written correspondence. Entries in the credit file that are being disputed should be circled. Supporting documentation should be coded to match entries circled in the credit file. All materials included in a written request should be sent via certified mail, return receipt requested, so that delivery of the correspondence is tracked and recorded.

Initiate an Investigation

Credit reporting agencies have a responsibility to investigate any disputed information promptly through the source of such information. If the investigation results in the agency's confirming the information as accurate, the agency must document the results in writing and provide such documentation to the disputing consumer. The consumer may then initiate a second investigation. If the investigations fail to resolve the dispute, the individual may document any discrepancies and include such documentation with his or her credit file. Such consumer input to a credit file is limited to 100 characters.

Under the FCRA, a credit reporting agency must forward the dispute to the creditor. In return, the creditor must investigate the dispute within 30 days of a request by reviewing all relevant information provided by the consumer reporting agency and send its findings back to the credit reporting agency. If the disputed information is found to be incorrect or inaccurate, the results must be reported to all nationwide credit reporting agencies that the creditor furnished the information to and all credit reporting agencies that compile and maintain files on a nationwide basis.

If no work is performed within 30 days of initiating the dispute, the credit reporting agency and the creditor or collector who provided the inaccurate information may be sued for willfully ignoring one's request. For each 30 day period that no work is performed, the more willful and intentional the credit reporting agency appears in a court of law. Though it is not required, individuals are encouraged to re-send the letter of request every 30 days via certified mail, return receipt requested, to document the passage of time. The initial 30 day ignorance is sufficient to establish liability, but any subsequent letters will increase the liability. Subsequently sent requests should have the terms,

"Second Request," "Third Request," marked across the top of the first page. In essence, the longer one's request is ignored, the more likely the individual is to receive monetary damages if he or she is successful in winning a legal suit.

If disputed entries are found to be in error, the credit reporting agency is required to correct the information and notify all nationwide credit reporting agencies of the correction. If disputed information is outdated, the credit reporting agency must update the information. If information is found to be unverifiable or belonging to another person, the credit reporting agency must delete the information. Credit reporting agencies are also required to delete accurate information if it represents negative information and is more than seven years old or, in the case of bankruptcy information, more than ten years old.

Once the investigation is complete, the credit reporting agency is required to send the consumer written notice of any actions taken with regard to the dispute. If the consumer disagrees with the findings, the consumer is allowed to question how the investigation was conducted and who was contacted for the investigation and add a statement to his or her credit file stating why they disagree. The credit-reporting agency is required to provide the consumer a free copy of the credit file if it was modified. The consumer then has the right to request that a corrected version of his or her credit report be sent to anyone who requested a report in the past six months. Information that is modified or removed cannot be put back into one's credit file unless the creditor who provided the information verifies that it is accurate and complete. In this case, the credit reporting agency must provide the consumer with written notice of the name, address, and telephone number of the creditor who verified the information.

If the investigation necessitates a correction to one's credit file and the credit reporting agency fails to correct the credit file within 30 days, the credit reporting agency may be sued for the disputed accuracy. Since a lawyer is necessary for representation in litigation, the law allows for disputing individuals to recover attorney fees and other costs in a successful lawsuit. If the disputing individual is forced to pay higher interest rates because of inaccuracies, the excess interest may be recovered as actual damage. If the credit reporting agency is found to fail willfully and intentionally to act on the disputed information, the disputing individual may also recover punitive damages.

Lawsuits regarding these types of disputes are best handled by an attorney who is trained in consumer issues. The National Consumer Law Center in Boston, Massachusetts, **http://www.nclc.org/** or the National Association of Consumers Advocates, **http://www.naca.net/** may provide individuals with contact information for attorneys who belong to these groups. These consumer advocate groups do not receive funding from the credit industry and it is expected that they will provide unbiased advice and contact information for attorneys who are able to provide proper representation.

CREDIT FURNISHER ERRORS

Consumers may contact creditors and collection agencies prior to contacting the credit reporting agency to allow the creditor or collection agency an opportunity to correct any errors and submit an update to the credit reporting agency before the credit reporting agency begins the process of investigating and verifying disputed entries.

Some states allow the disputing individual to sue both the credit reporting agency and the creditor who furnished the inaccurate information. Some states limit suits to credit reporting agencies. All states, however, allow disputing individuals to sue debt collectors. A suit against a debt collector does not require that one wait through the 30 day period, nor does it necessitate sending them a letter.

Find and Correct Credit Report Omissions

The law allows an individual to add information to a credit file if it is believed that the information would improve one's credit rating. Additional information may include loan repayments, salary increases, and good credit ratings established with companies that do not report to credit reporting agencies. When an individual requests that a credit reporting agency add account information that is not already listed in a credit file, the credit reporting agency may charge a fee to include the information. Some creditors only report and update information provided to specific credit reporting agencies. A creditor has no obligation to update account information that credit reporting agencies are requested to add to credit files.

Find and Correct Check Registry Errors

Check registries are those specialty consumer reporting agencies that track consumers' use of their checking account. Check registries maintain databases of consumer checking information, but banking institutions only report the negative activity. As with credit files that are maintained by credit reporting agencies, check registry files may contain incorrect and inaccurate checking information. The regulations of the FCRA and the FACT Act govern check registries. If a consumer's check is declined or the consumer is denied a bank account, the consumer is entitled to a free check registry report from the check registry that provided the report to the creditor or business entity that refused them. In addition, consumers are entitled to dispute information in check registry files in much the same manner as they are allowed to dispute entries in credit files.

The process for initiating a dispute is much the same, except that disputes must be submitted in writing and delivered via postal mail. The registry must initiate an investigation and verify the accuracy of disputed information, or the information must be removed within 30 days of receiving the dispute. It must correct any errors found and remove all outdated information. If the dispute does not result in a change to the disputed information, the consumer may add a 100 word statement to the check registry file that explains the circumstances. Most entries may be reported for up to seven years, but consumers may request removal five years from the reported date. An entry for an insufficient funds check may remain in a consumer's file indefinitely, but the entry must be marked as paid if payment is made for the check.

Establish a Credit Repair Plan

Any efforts made to pay down bills, take a second job, engage credit counseling, or file bankruptcy should be included in a credit repair plan, and the individual must then be responsible for acting on the planned activities. A credit repair plan should establish financial goals that indicate methods for spending and saving money in the near and far future. The credit repair plan should include a budget that is based realistically on the amount of income an individual has to work with. From that income, money should be allocated to the following:

- Necessary living expenses.

- Outstanding debts, such that they may be paid off as soon as possible.

- A savings plan to be used in emergency situations, such as illness or a loss of employment.

- A savings plan to be used in meeting established financial goals.

GOALS

Goals may be divided into four categories. They include short-term, intermediate-term, long-term, and life goals. Short-term goals are goals that are expected to be achievable within one year; intermediate goals are within the next five years; and long-term goals are more than five years. Life goals have no time limitation and may never really be achieved. Of the four categories of goals, life goals are the only goals for which money is not necessarily a factor. Life goals are more aspiration driven and may include things such as freedom and independence. The other types of goals have a time limit for completion.

One should establish short, intermediate, and long-term goals for one's finances. Goals should be categorized as such and then put in chronological order according to one's means, motive, and opportunity. Once goals are categorized, certain goals may be found to be too challenging and create frustration. Difficult or long-term goals may need to be broken down into more manageable stages to build on successes as one reaches the individual stages in an effort to meet the ultimate goal. If goals require a large amount of funds, they may be phased in over time rather than trying to achieve the final goal in one step. The various stages and phases in the process of achieving goals should be recognized and celebrated as an accomplishment.

Listing goals in chronological order means that one will have to determine which goals matter the most and concentrate on those goals that offer the most benefit, considering the circumstances and situations of the individual. It does not mean that one has to abandon certain goals, but it does require that those less important goals be put on the back burner until circumstances and conditions change so that one will be capable of focusing on them properly. Any plan or goal requires minor or major changes as circumstances change. Having stages and phases in the process of achieving goals provides checkpoints that allow one to evaluate progress at the end of each phase or stage and determine what, if any, changes may be incorporated. An unexpected lottery winning will have the effect of advancing the time line for goals. On the other hand, a job loss or layoff may have the effect of delaying the time line for goals. One must be prepared to adjust the plan for goals accordingly.

INCOME

One's income includes salary, overtime, bonuses, tips, and royalties. Income also includes money received from child support, alimony, investments, royalties, and rental property income. Consumers must be sure to establish their income as the amount of take home (net) pay, not their gross pay. Certain payroll deductions such as deductions for contributions to social security; federal, state, and local taxes; and contributions to retirement plans may be modified to increase one's net pay and disposable income. If excess money is being withheld from one's net pay such that one receives large state and/or federal tax refunds, the amount of the withholding may be reduced to produce more income to be used for paying expenses or debts. Taxpayers must be sure not to reduce their withholdings so as to create a penalty for underpaying taxes. Taxpayers should consult with someone experienced with tax matters to determine a suitable deduction.

EXPENSES

Living expenses include daily, weekly, and monthly financial commitments. They include expenses for food, shelter, clothing, and nonessential items. It is best to calculate income and expenses on a monthly basis because most expenses are paid on a monthly basis.

Acting on a credit repair plan begins with cutting expenses and freeing up cash that could be spent on repairing one's credit. Expenses that may be considered for trimming include the following:

- **Eating in and packing a lunch** rather than dining out may cut food expenses.

- **Shopping for essential needs** rather than nonessential items that one wants may reduce shopping expenses. Shopping as a form of entertainment and shopping addictions often lead to unplanned and unnecessary expenses.

- **Entertainment Forums** such as movie theaters, sporting events, concerts, plays costly when the cost of admission, travel, food, and drinks is included. Consumers should seek free forums of entertainment and use systems of home entertainment, such as television, videos, and movie rentals for viewing sports events and movies.

- **Hobbies that are inexpensive** should be substituted for expensive hobbies unless the hobby is a source of cash.

- **Cellular phones and home phones** may be converted to less expensive plans, or multiple phone services could be combined into a single service.

- **Cable service** may be converted to a less expensive service, though it may offer fewer channel options. Reading, talking, and other types of inexpensive activities may be substituted.

- **Eliminate some vehicle trip**s and do more walking.

- **Reduce water and energy use** by reducing thermostat temperatures on water heaters and furnaces. Follow instructions and recommendations offered by utility companies and make use of more energy efficient, cost cutting devices

- **If consumers receive a tax refund each year**, particularly those who receive a large refund, they may consider increasing their tax withholding deductions to make use of disposable income during the year. If necessary, they may also temporarily reduce or halt 401(K) deductions, though this is not recommended.

In calculating expenses, not all expenses require payment on a monthly basis. Consumers should prorate such expenses to a monthly amount. If the property tax on one's home is $1,600 per year, the expense should be prorated to a monthly expense by dividing the amount by 12, as follows:

$$\$1600 \div 12 \text{ months} = \$133.33 \text{ per month.}$$

Other types of expenses, such as food and entertainment vary from month to month. These types of expenses should be tallied over several months and then averaged. As an example, the grocery bill for a family averages $248 for the previous 6 months as follows:

	AMOUNT
Month 1	246.87
Month 2	283.74
Month 3	254.95
Month 4	236.97
Month 5	265.68
Month 6	199.76
Sum of Monthly Bills	1,487.97
Average Monthly Bill	248.99

Sum of Monthly bills ÷ 6 months = Average Monthly Bill

$1487.97 ÷ 6 months = $248.00

Incidental expenses that may be cut, reduced, or budgeted for include toiletries, car washes, dry cleaning, pet care, laundry, tobacco, children's allowances, gambling, day care, and others.

SAVINGS

Most people forget to include savings in their budget. A credit repair plan should include both a savings plan to meet financial goals and a savings plan for emergency situations. Savings should be included as an additional expense that needs to be paid monthly. It may be convenient to label the expenses as "self" or "us" and then pay that person or those persons each month by placing the expense amount in a separate savings account. As a monthly practice, the money becomes transparent and the savings accounts begin to grow. The same routine may be used for both types of savings.

A savings plan to meet financial goals should be established to finance the purchase of items or resources necessary in achieving established future goals. The savings may be used for the down payment on a home, a new vehicle, a vacation, or some other item. If the goal is to purchase a new vehicle and have $2,000 readily available to apply toward the down payment, tags, title, and other costs of purchasing a new vehicle, a savings plan should specify the amount of monthly savings required to reach that goal of $2,000. If the intention is to reach that goal within three years, one needs to establish a monthly savings amount of $56 over the next three years.

$$\$2,000 \div 36 \text{ months} = \$56$$

An adequate emergency savings account should include enough funds to cover six months or more worth of expenses. One should use the amount of expenses calculated when establishing a budget to determine how much to accumulate for the emergency savings account. If the budget calculations indicate monthly expenses of $1,750, it would take 53 months (less than five years) of saving $200 per month to fund an emergency savings account such that it covers six months worth of expenses.

$$\$1,750 \times 6 \text{ months} = \$10,500$$
$$\$200 \times 53 \text{ months} = \$10,600$$

TAX WITHHOLDINGS

In most cases of employment, the employer deducts income taxes for one's paycheck based on the number of deductions claimed by the employee. The deduction is an estimate of the expected taxes to be paid during the year. However, most people end up either paying additional tax because the amount was underestimated, or receiving a refund of the portion of the deduction that was overestimated by the employer. Other types of income are not subject to tax withholdings. Income from interest, dividends, tips, hobbies, rent, certain gifts, stocks gains, gambling winnings as well as income earned by independent contractors, small businesses, and landlords are not subject to tax withholdings.

Many workers boast about the large tax refund that they receive from the government each year as though the government were presenting them with a gift. The reality of this situation is that they have used their hard earned income to play lender to the government and at the end of the tax year, the government refunds the money that they borrowed. These workers "play" lender because real lenders charge interest on any amount borrowed, but workers are not allowed to apply interest to the money they lend to the government. The government refunds the borrowed money, interest-free. In addition, the government refunds the money at the end of the tax year, so that the worker may not request or receive any portion of the borrowed money before that time even if it were needed for an emergency.

Most workers would make better use of this money by applying it to their credit plan. It may be used to pay monthly expenses and debts. It may also be used to build savings and be readily available during the tax year, not when the government decides to reissue it.

Workers who lend money to the government and receive a refund each year, particularly those who receive a large refund, should consult with a qualified tax professional to determine how much withholding is necessary to pay their taxes without significantly overpaying or underpaying the tax.

A tax refund means that one has overpaid the required income tax. If one is required to pay income taxes at the end of the tax year, it means that they have underpaid the required tax on their income. While no one will be capable of determining the exact amount of income tax that will be due until all of the figures that are used to calculate income taxes are totaled, tax professionals will be capable of determining a withholding amount that puts one in a range of the required tax without significantly overpaying or underpaying the tax amount. A good practice is to seek a range in excess of $600 of the amount anticipated to ensure that the tax amount is slightly overpaid, or for those who prefer to pay at the end of the tax year, seek a range no less than $600 of the anticipated amount. While the IRS allows for overpayments and underpayments of the required tax, they will assess a penalty against excessive overpayments and underpayments.

ADDING INFORMATION TO A CREDIT REPORT

A good credit repair plan should include making payments on time and paying the full amount due each month so that positive information is included in one's credit report. Individuals should request that accounts in good standing, which are not already included in one's credit report, be included. The credit reporting company may require a fee to do this, but the fee may prove to be a small price to pay to improve one's credit. Opening new types of credit accounts that do not already exist in a credit report may prove useful as creditors examine the types of accounts when profiling potential customers. Consumers must be careful not to establish lines of credit that are so large that their calculated amount of available credit is not pushed beyond limits that are acceptable to creditors.

The 100 Word Statement

Consumers may also include a 100 word statement to rebut certain negative entries in their credit files. This statement is used to inform lenders, underwriters, and others who may access their credit report of the circumstances surrounding the information. The statement might be used to explain the consumer's position, such as the refusal to pay for defective products, inferior service, or the credit reporting agency's refusal to remove information that the consumer believes to be inaccurate or incorrect. The statement may also be used to explain late payments, charge-offs, or collections that resulted from an illness, job loss, or divorce. These statements are used strictly to communicate with the person reading the credit report. The statements have no impact on the calculation of one's credit score. Consumers may want to contact TransUnion about constructing such statements. TransUnion provides consumers with assistance in writing these statements. Consumers need to make sure that the statement remains applicable to current entries in their credit report. If a negative entry is removed or modified, the statement becomes outdated and it should be removed accordingly. An outdated statement that refers to past negative entries that are best forgotten is likely to do more harm than good.

RATE SHOPPING FOR MORTGAGE AND AUTO LOANS

When consumers are shopping for mortgages or auto loans, they may apply with multiple lenders to find the best deal on interest rates. These applications cause multiple lenders to create inquiries in their credit reports even though the consumer will eventually end up with only one loan. This specific type of borrowing behavior is realized in the credit reporting industry. The industry makes special consideration for multiple mortgages and auto loan inquiries when calculating credit scores. Multiple auto or mortgage loan inquiries made within a 14 day period are counted as a single inquiry when calculating one's credit score. Credit scores also do not consider mortgage and vehicle inquiries that are more than 30 days old. As such, consumers should attempt to rate shop for 14 day intervals or make a decision on a loan within 30 days to prevent multiple inquiries from affecting their credit score calculation.

Establish a Dialogue with Creditors

Individuals should contact creditors as soon as they foresee a problem with making timely payments to negotiate a more achievable payment schedule and to request that they keep at least a portion of late notations off credit reports. Creditors have more of an interest in collecting money due them than destroying one's credit. Contact may be made by telephone, in writing, by e-mail, or through links established on the creditor's Web site. Individuals should be positive in their conversions. They should be sure to get the person's name that they are communicating with and use the person's name rather than making reference to "you", "y'all," or "you people." Individuals should be clear and brief in explaining their situations and stick to the facts. If the situation revolves around a job loss or illness, it should be indicated without giving detailed and emotional commentary. After the situation has been indicated, the consumer should then offer a solution. The offer should accomplish the following:

- Indicate that a plan has already been established to resolve the problem immediately.

- Provide an estimate of the length of time needed to implement the plan and correct the problem. Even when an individual is not sure of the needed time frame, a realistic estimate must be identified. In any case, "I don't know" should not be used.

- Propose a payment plan and payment amount that is achievable before the creditor has a chance to propose a plan and amount that is unachievable.

Secured creditors, such as mortgage lenders, may appear to be less demanding than creditors of unsecured credit, such as credit cards companies, simply because they can be. Secured lenders are likely to make verbal contact in a more calm and polite manner or send what appears to be a non-threatening request for payment. However, the consequences of default are more severe since secured lenders are in a position to take possession of any collateral that secures the loan.

If individuals need to skip a payment, the creditor may be willing to allow it so long as the missed payment is recovered in the next month or two. If three or more months are required to get on track, the creditor may allow it, but the creditor may also close the account, which has a negative impact on the consumer's credit score. If the source of financial problems is a student loan, a short-term waiver may be acquired for certain circumstances if the lender is contacted before default. If more long-term solutions are required, consumers should negotiate for participation in a forbearance program or reduced payment schedule.

NEGOTIATE A FORBEARANCE PROGRAM

Some creditors have forbearance programs or hardship programs with pre-approved policies to assist customers with problems. Problems may include periods of unemployment, taking a low salaried job, illness, or returning to school. Consumers should contact the creditor to inquire about enrolling in a forbearance program. The contact person must follow specific channels to get approval from someone with more authority. After making an initial offer, the consumer may have to negotiate with the creditor to arrive at a workable solution. After the terms of a forbearance program have been established and agreed upon, the consumer should request written documentation confirming the new payment terms.

NEGOTIATE A REDUCED PAYMENT SCHEDULE

Creditors generally do not want individuals to default on their loan payments and may assist individuals in establishing a reduced payment schedule. Reduced payments should eliminate the need to make negative entries on one's credit report in the future for as long any newly negotiated plan is adhered to. Even when a debt has been sent to a collection agency, individuals may still negotiate with the creditor because negotiation puts the creditor in a position to recover the debt without having to pay the large commission usually required of debt collectors.

Consumers must be careful not to agree to any payment schedule that they cannot keep. When necessary, the consumer must indicate that a proposed solution is not possible and provide an explanation for the impossibility. When negotiations cannot be established with a particular customer service agent, the consumer should request to speak to a supervisor who may be more lenient in bending the rules.

Pay Bills on Time

Late payments play a major role in driving down one's credit score. Credit reports should indicate debts that have been paid on time and debts that have been paid in full. Any past due bills should be brought current and remain current. Paying bills on time has the effect of keeping bad credit from getting worse.

Seek Credit Counseling

If financial problems are severe, individuals should seek the services of a legitimate, nonprofit credit counseling service and avoid the scams that promise a quick reversal of credit scores. If an individual is behind on mortgage payments, the mortgage company will accept payment so long as the payment is made within the grace period specified in the mortgage loan documentation. However, if the grace period has passed, some states may require that the full amount of the current and past payments be made, and they do not have to accept any partial payment for the debt. In this situation, the consumer should seek the services of a credit counseling service. Credit counseling services may have more power in correcting this and other types of situations.

DEALING WITH DEBT COLLECTORS

Creditors have in-house collectors who attempt to collect delinquent debts. Creditors also sell debts to debt collectors when they are convinced that they will not be capable of collecting on a debt. Either debt collectors purchase debts for a fraction of the amount of the debt, or they assume the collection of debts in return for a commission on the amount that they are able to recover. If debt collectors are successful in recovering a debt from the debtor, the debt collector makes a generous profit from the purchase of the debt or generous commission for the debt recovery. To make a profit, debt collectors have resorted to some unscrupulous, unethical, and often illegal behavior to collect a debt. Recognizing the problems with debt collectors, the U.S. government established the Fair Debt Collection Practices Act (FDCPA) as an amendment to the Consumer Protection Act. The

FDCPA regulates the practices of debt collectors and prohibits the abusive practices of bullying and intimidation that debt collectors have used in the past. The FDCPA applies only to debt collectors that are unrelated to the original debt, purchase debts for profit, or receive a commission for collecting a debt. It does not apply to a creditor's in-house collectors. State laws established in states where creditors do business govern in-house collections. However, many creditors follow the FDCPA's rules in establishing their in-house collection procedures.

What Debt Collectors May Not Do

A debt collector may not use threatening, obscene, or abusive language when contacting a debtor, either verbally or in writing. Debt collectors are required to communicate in a business-like manner, and they may not annoy debtors with repetitive or excessively frequent communications. Debt collectors are prohibited from making idle threats that they will not or cannot carry out. A debt collector may not threaten court action if they do not intend to take the matter to court. Debt collectors cannot deceive debtors into thinking they are someone other than collectors attempting to collect a debt. They may not disguise themselves as inspectors or surveyors in an attempt to gain access to debtors. Debt collectors may not exaggerate the consequences of failing to pay a debt and threaten debtors with arrest or incarceration. Federal laws prohibit consumers from being jailed and imprisoned for failing to pay a debt.

What Debt Collectors May Do

The FDCPA specifies procedures and restrictions that govern what third-party debt collectors may and may not do. Debt collectors may engage in the following activities:

CONTACT

After contacting a debtor by phone, debt collectors must send the debtor notification within five working days of the attempt to collect the debt. The notification must indicate the name of the creditor who referred the debt to them, the amount of the outstanding debt, and the debtors' right to dispute the debt within 30 days of receipt of the notification, as well as language that indicates that any information obtained from the debtor will be used to satisfy the debt.

Debt collectors may contact debtors by phone between the hours of 8 a.m. and 9 p.m. They must receive permission from the debtor to make phone contact outside of these hours. Debt collectors may contact debtors directly in an effort to collect a debt unless the debtor directs them to contact their attorney, in which case the debtor must provide the debt collector with the contact information for the attorney. Debtors may request that they not be contacted in reference to the matter. If such a request is made, the debt collector is likely to refer the matter to a collection attorney. Debt collectors may contact debtors at work unless the debtor indicates that his or her employer prohibits it. They may contact debtors by postal mail so long as the outside of the correspondence does indicate an attempt to collect a debt. Postcards are prohibited. Debt collectors may contact other persons in an attempt to gather information on where a debtor lives and works. The contact may not be used to discuss the debt. Should these other persons inquire about who the debt collectors are, debt collectors may limit their response to their name or the name of their employers.

ENFORCE THE FINE PRINT

Debt collectors usually make use of the fine print attached to the original contract for a debt. The language of this print allows for fees and collection costs to be added to the debt amount. Other language of the original contract may allow a penalty rate to be applied to the original interest rate, significantly raising the interest rate applied to the debt. The fine print may also allow creditors to repossess purchases made with the debt amount. In most instances, the repossessed items only provide for a partial payment of the debt. The creditor determines the value of the repossessed item and may add the cost of reselling the item to the debt amount.

ACCEPT POST-DATED CHECKS

Some states allow debtors to request post-dated checks from debtors as payment. Post-dated checks eliminate the need to send payments in the future and ensure the collector that payment will be made on time and in the agreed amount. Though collectors are not supposed to cash post-dated checks before the posted date, some collectors do so. If this happens and sufficient funds are not in the debtor's checking account to cover the check, the check will bounce, creating even more debt for the debtor. Even if enough funds are in the debtor's checking account to cover the check, the early deposit of the post-dated check may cause an overdraft of the debtor's other checks or electronic purchases.

REPORT TO CREDIT REPORTING AGENCIES

Debt collectors have a right to report a debtor's delinquency to credit reporting agencies. Debt collectors may also take the matter to court in an attempt to obtain a legal judgment. In most cases, collectors consider a legal judgment more effective in satisfying a debt than repossessing any collateral of the debt. A judgment will attach to and damage the debtor's credit report. If not a legal judgment, collectors may damage a debtor's credit report with wage garnishment or a lien against any personal property.

ENGAGE A REVISION OF TERMS OR SETTLEMENT

Debt collectors may engage in a revision of the original contract terms if requested to do so by the debtor. The revised agreement should be provided in writing and usually allows the debt amount to be spread out among any future payments. Debt collectors may also offer or accept settlement of a lesser amount than the original debt. Any settlement should be stipulated in writing, and the debt collector is likely to require that the payment be made in a lump sum. In addition, the IRS taxes any amount forfeited in a settlement agreement as income to the debtor. Further, the debtor's credit report will indicate a settled payment, which has a negative effect on the debtor's credit rating.

Debt Collection Phone Calls

In response to phone calls from debt collection agencies, debtors should attempt to exercise control of the situation. A debt collector's primary interest is in collecting payment and finding out when and how a debtor intends to satisfy his or her debt. The FDCPA requires that debt collectors identify themselves and provide debtors with their real names. The act also requires that debtors identify their employer, if requested to do so. Debtors should be polite in requesting that debt collectors provide their first name, last name, the name of their employer, a mailing address, and their supervisor's name during the initial phone conversation. This information provides the debtor the contact information to use for written correspondence and complaints in the future. Debtors should also request that the debt collector provide evidence that the debt belongs to them. Debtors need to ensure that the debt collector is not making a mistake or that the debt collection attempt is not a scam. After the debt collector is able to provide proof that he or she is actually collecting on a debt of the debtor, the debtor may briefly explain his or her situation and offer a solution. The objective of the debtor should be to make an offer that he or she is able to commit to rather than waiting for the collector to demand payment or payments for certain amounts. The offer must include some method of paying the debt, usually over time. The offer may include monthly payments or bi-monthly payments for a predetermined amount of money. In some situations, a debt collector may not be willing to negotiate a solution and demand full payment or threaten court action, but debtors should not allow themselves to be pressured into a commitment that they will not be able to follow through on. Even if the matter ends up in court, the debtor's attempt to work out a solution may cause a judge to side with him or her. If an agreement for a payment plan is negotiated with the debt collector, the debtor must be sure to get the agreement in writing. If the debt collector does not draft the agreement, the debtor may draft the agreement and mail a certified copy of the agreement to the debt collector for signature. Even if the debt collector does not provide a signature, the debtor will have proof that the debt collector received the agreement.

FILING SUIT FOR INCORRECT AND INACCURATE INFORMATION

The three major credit-reporting agencies are private entities, not agencies of the U.S. government. The function of these private companies is to collect and sell information. As private companies, credit reporting agencies may be sued for damages when they fail to perform their jobs. When the information that is sold is inaccurate, the credit reporting agency may be sued in a court of law. Individuals may seek actual damages, punitive damages, attorney fees, and other costs. However, the agencies must first be notified that the information they are providing is inaccurate.

Creditors are responsible to report information to credit reporting agencies to be included in one's credit file. They may be sued for providing inaccurate information to the credit reporting agencies.

Debt collectors are also private companies that may be sued. Debt collectors are third-party companies that are unrelated to an original debt but attempt to collect the debt. Debt collectors purchase debts from creditors for pennies on the dollar, or they receive a commission for recovering debts and then attempt to collect on those debts for a profit. Many debt collectors may state that debts are assigned to them, but in actuality, debt collectors purchase debts or they are in a position to make a commission from recovered debts. Companies, including law firms, collect on purchased and commissioned debts. A law firm is only considered a debt collector if the firm collects debts as part of its regular business function. The Fair Debt Collection Practices Act (FDCPA) governs the practices of such law firms. Other law firms are not governed by the rules and regulations of the FDCPA in their attempts to collect a debt.

Many debt collection companies have resorted to unscrupulous and illegal behavior in their attempts to collect debts. The FDCPA establishes rules and regulations that debt collectors are required to comply with. The FDCPA is a strict liability law, which means debt collectors may offer few excuses for making a mistake. In fact, the only excuse that a debt collector may offer for making a mistake is that it was a bona fide mistake. However, if a consumer sends them a certified letter of dispute, even that defense fails. The FDCPA specifically states that a collection agency may not communicate or threaten to communicate credit information that is known or which should be known to be false, including failing to communicate that a disputed debt is, in fact, disputed. Debt collectors may be sued for actual damages as well as punitive damages of $1,000, costs, and attorney fees.

CHAPTER

CONSUMER CREDIT COUNSELING

Consumers who are overwhelmed with credit problems and unable to make progress in reducing their credit problems should engage the services of consumer credit counseling services before considering bankruptcy. This type of service may assist consumers in managing their debt loads and in establishing a credit repair plan that is unique to their particular situation. The information and knowledge gained through consumer credit counseling services is expected to assist consumers with both short-term and long-term credit problems. Consumers who choose to file for bankruptcy protection will be required to engage in this type of service before filing for protection anyway.

ACCREDITATION

The Council on Accreditation (COA) and the International Standards Organization (ISO) are responsible to accredit legitimate nonprofit credit counseling services. The COA is the largest third-party accrediting agency for non-profits in the nation. They specialize in accrediting nonprofit and government agencies that are located in the United States. The COA will perform a comprehensive agency-wide audit of a company's practices, policies, and safeguards before certifying them. The COA reviews boards of directors to ensure that they effectively promote the public over their own financial enrichment. Persons with expertise in the credit counseling business perform audits for the COA. The ISO is best known for standardizing manufacturing companies located around the world, but they also accredit nonprofit organizations using the same standards it uses for for-profit companies. The COA provides a more in-depth level of detail in its accreditation process than the ISO requires.

Some non-profits have no accreditation but serve to assist individuals and families with their finances and credit health. These non-profits must be selected carefully because so many so-called non-profits are scams. True non-profits should be affiliated with established organizations such as the United Way or government agencies, like the U.S. Department of Housing and Urban Development (HUD). Individuals should seek non-profits that are affiliated with organizations that have been established for at least ten years.

CERTIFICATION

While it is best to make use of credit counseling services that are accredited, credit counselors should also be independently certified by a third-party certifying organization. Individuals should check with the particular certifying authority to find out the standards they require for certification. In addition to being certified, credit counselors are expected to be professional and to provide individuals with basic courtesy. Though the office décor may not equal that of a professional law firm or a professional CPA firm, the level of professionalism provided by credit counselors should match that of such other professionals.

LEGITIMATE CREDIT COUNSELING SERVICES FEES

Legitimate credit counseling services do not charge up-front fees for their services. Any credit counseling agency that requires an up-front fee should be avoided, particularly those agencies that promise that in time an individual will be capable of earning back the fee. The timing and conditions specified for these types of deals make it unlikely that one will actually be capable of earning back the money. Legitimate nonprofit agencies will work with individuals for free or a nominal fee. Some agencies require a small initial fee while others require a small monthly fee. If debt management is recommended, these agencies may require a setup fee to establish a debt management plan. Nonprofit credit reporting agencies receive donations and grants from private individuals, businesses, and creditors to offset the cost of providing services.

It is estimated that about 75 percent of those who seek credit counseling arrive at a solution that meets their needs. The other 25 percent benefit from the establishment of a debt management plan. A debt management plan is an ongoing program that may take months to complete and usually requires participants to pay a monthly fee. Table 9 outlines some of reasonable charges that should be expected from a reputable credit counseling service. The costs do not include such things as the cost to obtain copies of one's credit report or the cost of educational materials that may be of assistance. In many instances, the necessity of these additions is optional.

Credit Counseling Services Fees	
Service	Range of Reasonable Fees
Credit Counseling	FREE to $50
Credit Counseling & One-Time Set-up Fee	FREE to $75
Monthly Debt Management Fee	$15 to $50

Table 9: Credit Counseling Fees

SERVICES OFFERED BY CREDIT COUNSELING SERVICES

Credit counselors should be willing to provide enough time during a counseling session to help an individual understand their financial problems and establish a plan and goals to rid them of the problems. Credit counseling sessions that last for less than an hour may be able to address surface issues, but they do not provide enough time to work with individuals to establish new goals, understand the source of the financial problems, or assist in figuring out a solution to the problems. Credit counselors should be willing to assist individuals in establishing new spending habits, a budget, financial goals, and a savings program. Credit counseling services will perform the following services:

- Detail what an individual owes.

- Develop an organized picture of one's financial situation.

- Advise individuals on steps necessary to reach their goals.

- Offer options that suit an individual's goals, resources, and lifestyle.

Initial contact with a credit counseling service involves detailed data gathering. Individuals will be required to disclose their monthly income sources, deductions, and expenses. The counseling session should include many questions relative to one's income, expenses, and debts. The amount of monthly income remaining after subtracting monthly expenses will be used to determine the amount of funds available, if any, to be used for monthly debt service. A credit counselor will suggest methods of generating a positive cash flow for one's household. A positive cash flow simply implies that more money comes into the household than goes out. The credit counselor will suggest methods of adjusting expenses and income to achieve a positive cash flow. If the amounts of income and expenses do not allow for a positive cash flow, the individual is referred to an attorney or other resource for additional help or legal assistance. If a positive cash flow is achievable, the debts of the household are assessed against the positive cash flow of the household. If any amount is left over from the positive cash flow after paying the household debts, the individual leaves with a workable spending plan and budget, along with a detailed analysis of their income and expenses. If no amount is left over, the expenses may be reworked and a debt service would have to be established under a debt management plan.

	Monthly Cash Flow = Monthly Income − Monthly Expenses		
	+	−	
Debt Service =Positive Cash Flow − Debts		Seek Legal or Other Sources of Assistance	
	+	−	
Establish Workable Spending Plan and Budget		Establish a Debt Management Plan	

Certified credit counselors are trained to offer options as part of the solution. They will balance what an individual needs to do, how long it will take to achieve established goals, and the types of resources available to assist the individual. Optional solutions should be provided in writing. Solutions, including bankruptcy, should be documented to deal with one's current financial situation as well as one's future needs. If the goal, for example, is to put the individual in a position to be able to purchase a home in the future, a good credit counselor will assist in developing a plan of action to address this future goal in addition to any immediate problems. The credit counselor should be capable of helping one understand how the financial condition occurred and what would be needed to correct it, while also maintaining a healthy financial reputation.

A useful action plan should also be documented to fit into the lifestyle of the individual. A budget designed to incorporate one's spending and saving style should be tailor-made to fit one's financial situation. It should not be composed of generalities taken from guidelines. Credit counselors should provide contacts to assist individuals beyond credit counseling and be open to individuals for additional suggestions as they move forward with any established plan.

Debt Management Plans

A debt management plan, also referred to as a debt repayment plan, requires that the credit counseling agency act as an intermediary in getting creditors to revise payments on behalf of the individual. For a monthly fee, they revise one's debt payments such that they are acceptable to creditors, leave the individual with enough money to pay living expenses, and get them out of debt within two to five years.

Creditors have come to realize that if individuals are not capable of paying debts, it is more beneficial for them to work with individuals through their credit counselors to get a return on their money than to receive no money should the individual file for bankruptcy protection. So long as creditors believe that the individual is not really capable of making payments as initially agreed, creditors may accept engaging in debt management plans which allow the credit counselor to apply a number of solutions, such as:

• **Revising monthly payments** to an amount that the individual can afford.

• **Stopping creditors from making collection calls.** The credit counseling agency is more than likely to convince creditors to stop calls made by collection companies. Some creditors will put an immediate halt to the calls as soon as a debt management plan is in place. Other creditors usually put an end to the calls after about three months of payments have been made. Rarely does a creditor allow the calls to continue after payments are made.

• **Stopping wage garnishments.** If a court action is pending to garnish wages, the action may move forward, but the action will end before any court order to garnish wages is actually issued.

• **Stretching out payments** so that balances are paid off in at least 60 months.

• **Reducing interest rates and any fees associated with loans**. The amount of reduction in interest rates is dependent upon the creditor, not the credit counseling agency. Some creditors follow strict corporate policies while others are allowed to offer concessions based on one's perceived need. However, the credit counseling agency will have more influence with creditors in negotiating a reduction than an individual would be capable of achieving alone. Consumers should expect that some creditors would be willing to accept a large reduction while others will only accept a small reduction. The agency also has the influence to have late charges and over-the-limit fees waived after a debt management plan is established.

While a debt management plan may assist with such things as lowering interest rates paid to creditors or reducing monthly payment amounts, these plans offer some disadvantages as well. Disadvantages include the following:

- Difficulty in switching credit counselors after beginning the plan.

- Negative entries on one's credit file.

- An increase in interest rates.

- Restricted access to new credit during the terms of the plan.

Debt management will not clear negative entries from one's credit file. Debt management will assist in the renegotiation of the terms of debt before creditors have cause to include negative information in one's credit file. However, a debt management counselor may assist an individual in clearing negative entries from credit files that are inaccurate.

If one's credit file shows negative entries, a debt management counselor may assist in cleaning up the credit file and reducing the debt load faster. As an example, John is six months behind on a $150 monthly payment to a creditor. John's billing statement indicates that he owes in excess of $1,050 (monthly payment amount and other fees) on the debt and his credit file shows that he is six months late. Federal regulations provide for a creditor to re-age accounts for good reason, every five years. When an account is re-aged, it is brought up to current or paid-as-agreed status. Creditors usually require the full amount of any outstanding balance to be paid and three consecutive payments to be made on time before they will report one's account as current. Three consecutive payments under a debt management plan are considered a good reason for re-aging an account, even when an account is more than three payments behind. If John were to engage a debt management firm, he would benefit by having a newly agreed upon reduction in monthly payments and a reduction in the applicable interest rate. In addition, any late fees and over-the-limit fees may be eliminated. After three payments of the newly agreed upon monthly payment, John's account would be reported as current. If on the other hand, John did not engage in debt management, he would have to pay the outstanding $1,050, incurred late fees, any other fees incurred, and then make three consecutive payments of $150 on time before the creditor would report his account as current.

With Debt Management	Without Debt Management
Reduction in payments.	Total outstanding balance.
Reduction in interest rates.	Interest.
Late fees waived.	Late fees.
Over–the-limit fees waived.	Other fees.

Debt Settlement Plans

A debt settlement plan differs greatly from debt management plans offered by some credit counseling services. Though the two are often confused as being same, they are not. A debt settlement plan requires that an individual pay money to a company that will hold that money until the creditor gives up on trying to recover payment and, supposedly, is willing to accept a settlement for a lesser amount. Even if the process were to work, one's credit would be severely damaged for years into the future. Furthermore, the amount forgiven in the settlement would become taxable as income to the individual. The IRS taxes the forgiven amount and the tax debt owed to the IRS remains binding even if the individual decides to file bankruptcy in the future. Another nuance of debt settlement companies is that they have a tendency to keep all of the payments made to them if one defaults on just one payment.

CREDIT COUNSELING SCAMS

There are many companies that advertise credit counseling services, but it is not possible for them to provide the services that they claim. Most companies use confusing terminology in their advertisements to lure consumers into thinking that they are providing legitimate services. Some of tricky language of advertising follows:

- **Not-for-profit**. This term is often used because it is easily confused with the term, nonprofit. Not-for-profit does not mean inexpensive or honest.

- **Debt free**.

- **Get out debt without repaying creditors**. The company may offer a settlement program, but the company's settlement program is not likely to account for secured debts, such as mortgages, child support, and student loans, among others.

- **Erase all your debts** and save thousands of dollars.

- **Money in your pocket** at the end of the month.

- **Stop** embarrassing collection calls now.

- **Reduce debt** up to 60 percent in seconds.

- **IRS 501(C)(3) approved**. This advertisement does not represent any type of approval by the IRS. It simply means that the company reported to the IRS that the company qualified for tax exemption under the tax code. It does not indicate whether the IRS agreed with the decision to make such a report.

- **Established relationships with creditors**. Anyone who pays a creditor has established a relationship with that particular creditor. This terminology does not signify that the company's relationship with creditors will be of any benefit to the consumer.

REFERRALS FOR CREDIT COUNSELING SERVICES

Consumers may check with the credit counseling accrediting organizations for prospective credit counseling agencies. The ISO is found at **www.iso.com** and the COA may be found at **www.coanet.org.** Accreditation signifies that a client's funds will be handled appropriately, the agency is licensed to conduct business in the particular state, and the agency maintains a trained and certified staff. Consumers must be sure to check that any claimed accreditation is current and not based on criteria from years past.

Consumers may seek references from their state's consumer

protection office, which may provide information about complaints and legal actions, if any, filed against local credit counseling agencies.

The Better Business Bureau (BBB) is also a good source of information about credit counseling services. Complaints are likely to be filed with the BBB, but the BBB also provides dispute resolution histories, consumer information advisories, and regulatory actions taken against or pending against companies. The BBB should be able to assist consumers in determining the number of complaints and the resolution of such complaints.

The Internet is useful in providing consumers with access to a wealth of information about various companies. The GuideStar Web site, located at **www.guidestar.org**, provides information on more than one million nonprofit organizations. GuideStar is funded by a number of big names in foundations in the United States, and GuideStar has provided this type of service for more than a decade. GuideStar will provide financial summaries, names of boards of directors, and IRS tax returns for companies. Consumers should be cautious of companies that provide excessive salaries for top management as compared to other similar sized companies, indications of much more revenue than expenses, payrolls that include relatives of management and private companies that receive large payments or are owned by top management.

CHAPTER

7

IDENTITY THEFT

Identity theft occurs when someone pretends to be someone else for financial gain. A person who makes use of another person's credit card number, address, birth date, social security number, or account number or uses their user name or password to open lines of credit or new accounts is an identity thief, and an identity thief is a criminal. These criminals steal mail from mailboxes, sift receipts from trash, hack into computer systems, steal documents from homes, or whatever it takes to get their hands on personal information that may be of use in committing crimes.

Contrary to the popular belief that identity theft results from electronic transactions, statistics indicate that most cases of identity theft occur from paper. In the year 2004, the most frequently reported cause of identity theft was the loss of a wallet or checkbook. The top five causes of identity theft are as follows:

- Lost or stolen wallet or checkbook.

- Relatives, friends, and associates.

- Corrupt employees.

- Offline transactions.

- Stolen snail mail.

Consequently, persons who are known to identity theft victims are responsible for committing half of all cases of identity theft. In many instances, identity theft victims do not know they have been victimized until their credit has been damaged, they are turned down for credit, or they begin to receive collection calls.

After an account has been compromised, one should change all PINs, user names, passwords, and account numbers. To change account numbers, one must close an existing account and open a new account. Credit card accounts, bank accounts, and other accounts should be closed and reopened. Longer passwords and those that include a combination of numbers and characters are harder for hackers to figure out. Consumers should be creative in selecting passwords so that they are also relatively easy to remember when needed.

Consumers are consistently encouraged to engage in electronic transactions because of the safety and security inherent in electronic systems. Financial transactions and information transfers are much safer using electronic transfer systems, accessed with user names, PINs, and passwords, than having them delivered via postal mail. It is still possible to become a victim of identity theft through the use of electronic mediums, but it is far safer than mail delivery and other manual systems. Consumers must protect their accounts from inaccuracies, mis-merged data, fraud, and identity theft. By safeguarding PIN numbers, signing cards immediately upon receipt, and shredding receipts, unused credit offers, and other documents that display personal information, one may reduce the probability of fraud.

Credit reporting agencies are allowed to share credit information with marketers who submit unsolicited offers. An individual may request that the three major reporting agencies not share such information with marketers. Requests may be made by calling 1-888-567-8688.

A common form of identity theft occurs when an ex-spouse establishes a credit account in the name of the other ex-spouse and has the bill sent to an address that is different from the other ex-spouse's address. The ex-spouse who fraudulently opens the account may run up the credit limit of the account, and the innocent ex-spouse never even sees the bill. By the time the innocent spouse becomes aware of the account, it is likely to be in collections and entered negatively on both of their credit reports. With this type of identity theft, the creditor may require that the innocent ex-spouse press charges against the fraudulent ex-spouse.

PHISHING

Phishing is also a common source of identity theft. It involves a stranger pretending to be someone else and using e-mail to request confirmations of critical account information. Phishing is also accomplished with the use of spyware. Spyware is on computer software programs that are either downloaded or uploaded to computer systems, usually without the computer user's consent, knowledge, or understanding. Some computer spyware is embedded in legitimate software that is purchased from vendors. By accepting the licensing agreement, which is supplied with virtually all software, one agrees to have additional software downloaded from the Internet or uploaded from the installation disk. Vendors understand that most people do not bother to read the licensing agreement that is supplied with software, or the language of the software agreement is such that one is not likely to understand even by reading it. Other spyware programs are secretly downloaded from the Internet simply by visiting certain Web sites.

Spyware programs do what the name implies: they spy on computer systems. Some programs perform keyboard captures, which means they capture everything that is typed during a computer session. That information is either transmitted over the Internet, if the user is online, or stored and saved in a file that is transmitted when an Internet connection occurs. Other spyware programs seek specific types of files that are stored on a computer system and send copies of those files over the Internet. Most of these types of programs take advantage of vulnerabilities in computer operating systems. They run in the background of the computer systems so that the user is not aware that the program is running. The following suggestions are offered to guard one's computer system against phishing scams.

- **Be suspicious of e-mails requesting personally identifying information, such as account numbers and passwords**. Legitimate companies will not request this type of information to be sent electronically through e-mail. They will request that consumers log onto their Web site or follow some other method to provide such information. E-mail systems cannot provide the type of security that may be built into Web sites.

- **Refuse to supply personal information over the Internet unless the source of the request for information can be confirmed and the Web site link is secure**. When a user is on a secure Web site a padlock icon appears on the browser page, usually in the lower right-hand corner of the page.

The address of secure sites should begin with https://. This is not to be confused with http:// (without the "s").

- **Be suspicious of e-mails that are not personalized with the correct name**. Users should not respond to e-mails addressed to "dear customer" or those addressed to someone else.

- **Never click on links embedded in e-mails from anyone who is unfamiliar**. Many times, perpetrators of spyware programs will link users to Web sites where the software may be secretly downloaded. In other cases, a link may download an infectious virus that will infect and harm the computer system.

- **Forward suspicious e-mails to the FYTC** at **spam@ucre.gov** and file a complaint with the Internet Fraud Complaint Center (IFCC) at **www.ifccfbi.gov**.

FRAUD ALERTS

Identity theft victims may place fraud alerts in their credit files to assist with preventing identity theft. Likewise, active duty military personnel serving away from their regular duty station, may place active duty alerts in their credit files to help prevent identity theft.

SECURITY FREEZES

Some states provide methods for consumers to place a security freeze in their credit files. A security freeze prevents credit reporting agencies from sharing information in one's credit file with newly inquiring creditors and other companies. A security freeze will not affect companies that the consumer already has an existing business relationship with. This is inclusive of collection agencies that act on behalf of creditors. Further, credit reports will be accessible for pre-screening credit offers. Security freezes were implemented to combat identity theft. However, a security freeze is not a 100 percent guarantee against identity theft, primarily because many businesses issue credit without pulling credit reports.

The law exempts certain parties from a security freeze and also exempts those parties that an individual requests exemption for. If a consumer applies for credit while their credit file is under a security freeze, that individual will need to contact each credit reporting agency to request a temporary relief of the security freeze or their credit application will be rejected. A request for temporary lift of a security freeze may take three or more business days to process. In addition, the request may not be initiated on non-business days, non-business hours, weekends, or holidays. Consumers may request a temporary lift of a security freeze for a specified date range. Only the consumer is allowed to make request for a security freeze, temporary lift of the security freeze, or a permanent removal the security freeze. A security freeze remains in effect until the consumer requests a permanent removal of the freeze.

Requests to initiate, temporarily remove, or permanently remove a security freeze must be made in writing and sent via certified mail to following addresses, as applicable.

Equifax	Experian	TransUnion
Security Freeze	P.O. Box 9554	Call 1-888-909-8872 to
P.O. Box 105788	Allen, Texas 75013	request an application that
Atlanta, Georgia 30348		specifies the mailing address.

The request must include the name, address, date of birth, and social security number of the requesting consumer. Proof of the current address must be documented with evidence such as a current utility bill. The consumer must include applicable fees, payable with a personal check, money order, or credit card as indicated in Table 9. If payment is made by credit card, the consumer must include the name that appears on the card, the type of credit card (American Express, MasterCard, VISA, or Discover Card), the complete account number, expiration date, and card identification number. For American Express cards, the four digit card identification number located on the front of card and above the account number should be used. For MasterCard, VISA, or Discover Cards, the three digit card identification number on back of card at the end of the account number should be used. Identity theft victims must include a copy of a police report, Identity Theft report, or other law enforcement agency report, such as a DMV report, with the request.

Upon receipt of a security freeze request and placement of the security freeze in a credit file, the credit reporting agency will send the consumer a confirmation letter via postal mail that contains a 10 digit security freeze confirmation number. This security freeze confirmation number will be required to make request for temporary lifts or the permanent removal of the security freeze. If the confirmation number is lost or forgotten, it will affect processing any requests to lift or remove the security freeze.

Unlike fraud alerts, a fee is required to initiate, suspend, or remove a security freeze from credit files. Fees are assessed by each credit reporting agency. However, victims of identity theft may obtain security freezes free of charge in most of the states where security freezes are offered. Security freezes were rejected as a federal requirement in the recently passed FCRA. Some states, however, make security freezes available to its residents as indicated in Table 10. The indicated fees are as specified by the Equifax credit reporting agency.

STATE	EFFECTIVE DATE	IDENTITY THEFT VICTIM	NON-VICTIM			
			INITIATE FREEZE	TEMPORARY REMOVAL (date range)	TEMPORARY REMOVAL (per creditor)	PERMANENT REMOVAL
California	1/1/2003	FREE	$10	$10	$12	FREE
Colorado	71/2006	FREE	FREE (1st Freeze) $10 (subsequent) freeze)	$10	$12	FREE
Connecticut	1/1/2006	FREE	$10	$10	$12	FREE
Florida	7/1/2006	FREE	$10	$10	N/A	FREE
Illinois	1/1/2006	FREE	N/A	N/A	N/A	N/A
Kentucky	7/11/2006	FREE	$10	$10	N/A	FREE
Louisiana	7/1/2005	FREE	$10	$8	N/A	FREE
Maine	2/1/2006	FREE	$10	$10	$12	FREE
Minnesota	8/1/2006	FREE	$5	$5	$5	FREE
Nevada	10/1/2005	FREE	$15	$18	$20	FREE
New Jersey	1/1/2006	FREE	FREE (1st freeze)	$5	$5	FREE
North Carolina	12/1/2005	FREE	$10	$10	N/A	FREE
South Dakota	7/1/2006	FREE	N/A	N/A	N/A	N/A
Texas	9/1/2003	$8	N/A	N/A	N/A	N/A
Vermont	7/1/2005	FREE	$10	$5	$5	FREE
Washington	7/24/2005	FREE	N/A	N/A	N/A	N/A
All Other States		N/A	N/A	N/A	N/A	N/A

Table 10: Security Freeze Fees

A security freeze request made to one major credit reporting agency in Texas must be honored by the other two major credit reporting agencies.

SAFEGUARDING CREDIT INFORMATION

For consumers to protect themselves from damage by unauthorized use of personal identifying information, consumers must check with various sources to verify the accuracy of any personal information made available.

The Social Security Administration (SSA) has historically allowed the change of social security numbers for persons in federal witness protection programs and victims of domestic violence. The same type of procedure may be used for victims of identity theft. The process is long and complicated and promises to become more complicated with the nation's emphasis on national security. Consumers must be prepared to oversee all necessary record changes personally because the government will not. Consumers may find more information about changing their social security numbers by contacting the SSA as follows:

Website:	www.socialsecurity.gov
Telephone:	1-800-772-1213
TTY for hearing impaired:	1-800-325-0778

Each state's Department of Motor Vehicles (DMV) will also allow for the change of a driver's license number. Consumers must check with state authorities to determine how to go about the process.

SAFEGUARDING COMPUTER SYSTEMS

- Keep laptops safe and do not let out of sight so that others will have no opportunity to steal them.

- Close computer files that contain personal information when away from the computer.

- Password protect computer systems and screen savers to prevent others from gaining access.

- It may be beneficial to keep a list of passwords but do not keep the list near the computer.

- Install a firewall on wireless computer networks and make sure that the firewall is encrypted.

- Install software that detects, controls, and/or protects computer systems from harmful viruses, spyware, and adware.

- Delete unnecessary and unused personal information from computer systems.

SAFEGUARDING POSTAL MAIL

- Convert financial business transactions and communications to online systems provide for online transactions over secure Web sites.

- Use locked mailboxes that only accept mail or use a post office box.

- Carry checks and other financial and personal information to the post office to be mailed rather than using a home mail box.

- Request the bank to hold new check orders until they can be picked up

CHAPTER

FILING BANKRUPTCY

Bankruptcy laws are designed to assist persons who invest in business or take other financial risks. If the business fails or the risk results in loss, bankruptcy provides protection from creditors' rights to collect on owed debt. Despite the negative stereotypes of persons who file bankruptcy (destitute, impoverished, financially ruined), bankruptcy is good for the economy. Without bankruptcy protection, the risk of borrowing money would be so high that few people would be willing to take advantage of borrowing, and borrowing governs the U.S. economy.

In seeking bankruptcy protection, one may request to keep some debts if they can prove to the court that they can afford to pay the debt. This is referred to as reaffirmation. Reaffirmation is good for those with short credit histories and it is also good for rebuilding credit scores. Part of the credit score calculation considers the age of accounts and longevity with creditors and may assist in increasing one's credit score. Consumers must be sure to keep debts that are truly affordable. They must ensure that the terms and conditions of the credit will not change due to the bankruptcy filing. It is possible that the creditor may reduce the available credit limit to the amount of the already outstanding debt and raise the interest rate to the maximum specified in the terms and conditions of the credit. In such a case, the higher interest may push the outstanding balance over the limit and cause more fees to be assessed against the account.

Bankruptcy protection provides a legal method for individuals and businesses to start over again after suffering a financial hardship. Without bankruptcy, some people and some businesses would never be capable of recovering from financial hardship and regaining a normal life. Bankruptcy allows protection from most creditors through the courts. By filing bankruptcy, the fees, penalties, and legal threats issued by creditors would be brought to a halt.

More than one million American families file for protection under bankruptcy codes each year. Studies indicate that divorced women who are responsible for raising their children are five times more likely to file bankruptcy than any other group. Of all of the cases of bankruptcy, more than half are reported to be a result of sudden uninsured medical expenses.

The bankruptcy code segments types of bankruptcy into chapters.

Chapter	Purpose
7	Liquidation
9	Municipalities, such as cities and counties
11	Companies
12	Farmers
13	Wage Earner

Among the various chapters of the bankruptcy code, the chapters most often used by consumers are Chapters 7 and 13. Chapter 7 of the bankruptcy code is known as liquidation. Consumers are required to liquidate some of their assets to be relieved of most of their debts. Chapter 13 of the bankruptcy code is known as wage-earner bankruptcy. The consumer is allowed to keep most assets and, under court protection and supervision, repay debts with a deadline from three to five years, and no interest is assessed on payments made. Federal laws govern the bankruptcy code; however, state laws are established for debtor-creditor relationships. As such, state laws govern the particular types of property and other exemptions that are included in asset liquidation.

Certain debts will not be relieved under bankruptcy codes. These debts must be paid regardless of a bankruptcy filing. They include the following:

- Federal, state, and local taxes.

- Alimony.

- Child support.

- Student loans.

- Debts owed as a result of drunk driving.

THE BANKRUPTCY ABUSE PREVENTION AND CONSUMER PROTECTION ACT (BAPCPA)

The growth and abuse of bankruptcy filings over the years led to Congress' passing the Bankruptcy Abuse Prevention and Consumer Protection Act (BAPCPA) in 2005 to impose restrictions on bankruptcy filings, and to prevent abuse. The BAPCPA specifies the following:

- **Before filing bankruptcy,** consumers are limited in their spending and borrowing behavior. Consumers may not have made substantial credit purchases, usually, within the 90 days before filing bankruptcy.

- **Before filing bankruptcy,** consumers are required to attend credit counseling from an approved nonprofit credit counseling agency. The trustee of the bankruptcy court maintains a listing of approved credit counseling agencies. Consumers may contact the clerk of the court who handles bankruptcies in their district to obtain a listing. Consumers may also contact either of the two largest networks of credit counseling agencies. They include the following:

The National Foundation for Credit Counseling	The Association of Independent Consumer Credit Counseling Agencies
www.nfcc.org	www.aiccca.org
1-800-388-2227	1-800-450-1794

An approved credit counseling agency must meet the following criteria established by Congress.

- Be a nonprofit organization.

- Charge reasonable fees and provide services to those who cannot afford to pay the fee.

- Train its counselors adequately.

- Not base counselors' pay on the outcome of counseling sessions.

- Provide adequate counseling including an analysis of the customer's current financial situation, an analysis of the circumstances that created their financial situation, and options to solve their problems without causing a negative amortization of debts. A negative amortization of debts occurs when payments toward debts are not sufficient to pay the interest and fees as well as pay down the principal. The debt continues to grow rather than being reduced.

- Disclose its funding sources.

- Disclose any costs incurred for services and how those costs are to be paid.

- Disclose the qualifications of counselors.

- Disclose the impact that counseling services have on credit histories.

- Have an independent board of directors where the majority of the board members are not employed by the agency.

- Have board members who do not financially benefit either directly or indirectly from the credit counseling sessions.

Consumers must provide creditors with a copy of their tax return if requested to do so. Consumers are required to provide their creditors with information about their finances so that creditors have written documentation of the inability to pay. Under Chapter 13, consumers are required to provide creditors with tax returns filed in the last four years. An attorney must certify that statements and information documented and presented to the courts are true.

Eligibility for Chapter 7 requires that consumers pass a means test that proves an inability to pay all or a portion of debts. The means test is used to determine whether the consumer qualifies to file for bankruptcy protection under Chapter 7 or Chapter 13 of the bankruptcy code. Under a Chapter 13 bankruptcy, all disposable income must be included in a debt repayment plan. Each year, the consumer's income and expenses must be documented to determine if more income can be applied to the debt repayment. Under Chapter 13, certain debts are designated as priority debts. Priority debts take precedence over all other debts and they must be paid in full. Payment to the trustee of the court for administrative fees to cover administering the Chapter 13 repayment plan takes precedence over all other debt repayments. Domestic support debts are second in priority.

Even though the federal court system handles cases of bankruptcy, states are allowed to limit the amount of homestead exemption that consumers may keep in a bankruptcy. Homestead exemption is the amount of equity in one's home that may be excluded from bankruptcy filings. If the home was purchased less than 40 months before the bankruptcy filing, the maximum exemption allowed is $125,000, regardless of the states's exemption allowance. This cap on the exemption is not applicable if the property was acquired prior to the 40 month period and it was transferred from a previous principal residence.

Bankruptcy will not prevent eviction if the consumer fails to pay rent, and certain debts must be paid regardless of a bankruptcy filing. Those debts include the following:

- Federal, state, and local taxes.

- Alimony.

- Child support.

- Student loans.

- Debts owed as a result of drunk driving.

After filing bankruptcy, but before a discharge of bankruptcy, consumers must complete a course in financial management. The trustee of the bankruptcy court must approve the course. The course may be taught by a credit counseling agency or the educational entity that is qualified by the court. All approved courses must be the following requirements:

- Provide experienced and trained instructors.

- Provide relevant teaching materials and teaching methodologies.

- Be offered in an adequate training facility, be provided over the telephone, or provided over the Internet.

- Consumers must wait a specified number of years after filing bankruptcy to file bankruptcy again. The BAPCPA specifies eight years for Chapter 7, two years Chapter 13 and four years between a Chapter 7 and 13 filing.

THE MEANS TEST AND QUALIFYING FOR PROTECTION UNDER CHAPTER 7

Chapter 7 bankruptcy protection has been the most popular form of bankruptcy filing in recent years because it effectively relieves consumers of the obligation to pay debts and the nuisance of dealing with debt collectors. The BAPCPA has placed new limitations and restrictions on Chapter 7 filing requirements. The new rules are designed to limit the abuse of Chapter 7 filings by ensuring that persons who are capable of paying all or part of their debt are put a position to do so. Under the new rules, consumers must pass a means test (of income) to determine if they qualify for bankruptcy protection under Chapter 7 or Chapter 13. The means test specifies that one may file for bankruptcy protection under Chapter 7 if they meet at least one of the three established tests.

The first test is to determine whether one's income is below the median established for their state of residence. Income is verified by submitting the most recent tax return to the bankruptcy court. Median income is based on family size and may easily be determined for one's family size and state of residence by accessing the spreadsheet on the Census Bureau Web site, located at **www.census.gov/hhes/www/income/medincsizeandstate.xls.**

Even if debtors' incomes are too high and they fail to meet the first test, they may still qualify for Chapter 7 bankruptcy protection if they meet the requirements of the second test.

The second test determines whether one's excess monthly income is under $166.66. The $166.66 amount is the excess income that the government specifies is enough to pay a $10,000 debt over five years.

$$166.66 \times 12\text{-months} \times 5\text{-years} = \$10,000$$

Interest is not applied to payment amounts made under bankruptcy so that the calculation does not account for any interest payments. If one is found to have an excess monthly income of at least $166.66, they will not be able to file for bankruptcy protection under Chapter 7; they must file for protection under Chapter 13.

The IRS establishes guidelines that determine how much of one's income will be considered excess income. The IRS publishes spending guidelines that specify allowances for certain expenses. After these allowances are deducted from one's income, the remaining income is considered excess. The monthly allowances are as listed in Table 11. The allowances may be found on the Department of Justice (DOJ) Web site, under IRS National Standards for Allowable Living Expenses, located at **www.usdoj.gov/ust/eo/bapcpa/bci_data/national_expensestandards.htm.** National standards are applicable throughout the United States except in Alaska and Hawaii, which have separate schedules because of their unique geographic circumstances and higher costs of living. Allowances for Alaska and Hawaii may also be found on the DOJ Web site.

One Person National Standards
Based on Gross Monthly Income

Item	Less than $833	$833 to $1,249	$1,250 to $1,666	$1,667 to $2,499	$2,500 to $3,333	$3,334 to $4,166	$4,167 to $5,833	$5,834 and over
Food	175	203	232	257	292	333	373	483
Housekeeping supplies	18	24	30	31	32	33	34	49
Apparel & services	47	48	62	68	89	104	140	217
Personal care products & services	17	24	27	32	33	41	46	57
Miscellaneous	110	110	110	110	110	110	110	110
Total	$367	$409	$461	$498	$556	$621	$703	$916

Bankruptcy Allowable Living Expenses – National Standards
(See 11 U.S.C. § 707(b)(2)(A)(ii)(I))

Food & Clothing (Apparel & services)*	222	251	294	325	381	437	513	700
5% of Food & Clothing	11	13	15	16	19	22	26	35

Two Persons National Standards
Based on Gross Monthly Income

Item	Less than $833	$833 to $1,249	$1,250 to $1,666	$1,667 to $2,499	$2,500 to $3,333	$3,334 to $4,166	$4,167 to $5,833	$5,834 and over
Food	305	306	322	368	418	460	514	723
Housekeeping supplies	27	33	42	43	50	51	55	85
Apparel & services	83	91	92	93	98	126	141	277
Personal care products & services	25	27	33	37	40	50	56	83
Miscellaneous	138	138	138	138	138	138	138	138
Total	$578	$595	$627	$679	$744	$825	$904	$1,306

Bankruptcy Allowable Living Expenses – National Standards
(See 11 U.S.C. § 707(b)(2)(A)(ii)(I))

Food & Clothing (Apparel & services)*	388	397	414	461	516	586	655	1,000
5% of Food & Clothing	19	20	21	23	26	29	33	50

Three Persons National Standards
Based on Gross Monthly Income

Item	Less than $833	$833 to $1,249	$1,250 to $1,666	$1,667 to $2,499	$2,500 to $3,333	$3,334 to $4,166	$4,167 to $5,833	$5,834 and over
Food	422	423	424	425	512	513	565	754
Housekeeping supplies	41	42	43	44	51	52	61	86
Apparel & services	143	144	145	146	154	155	168	278
Personal care products & services	30	33	34	38	41	51	57	84
Miscellaneous	166	166	166	166	166	166	166	166
Total	$802	$808	$812	$819	$924	$937	$1,017	$1,368

Bankruptcy Allowable Living Expenses – National Standards
(See 11 U.S.C. § 707(b)(2)(A)(ii)(I))

Food & Clothing (Apparel & services)*	565	567	569	571	666	668	733	1032
5% of Food & Clothing	28	28	28	29	33	33	37	52

Four Persons National Standards
Based on Gross Monthly Income

Item	Less than $833	$833 to $1,249	$1,250 to $1,666	$1,667 to $2,499	$2,500 to $3,333	$3,334 to $4,166	$4,167 to $5,833	$5,834 and over
Food	433	463	501	502	588	574	685	868
Housekeeping supplies	42	43	44	46	52	53	66	94
Apparel & services	144	145	151	152	190	191	201	302

Personal care products & services	44	46	47	48	49	52	58	89
Miscellaneous	193	193	193	193	193	193	193	193
Total	$856	$890	$936	$941	$1,042	$1,063	$1,203	$1,546

Bankruptcy Allowable Living Expenses – National Standards
(See 11 U.S.C. § 707(b)(2)(A)(ii)(I))

Food & Clothing (Apparel & services)*	577	608	652	654	748	765	886	1170
5% of Food & Clothing	29	30	33	33	37	38	44	59

More than Four Persons National Standards
Based on Gross Monthly Income

Item	Less than $833	$833 to $1,249	$1,250 to $1,666	$1,667 to $2,499	$2,500 to $3,333	$3,334 to $4,166	$4,167 to $5,833	$5,834 and over
For each additional person, add to four person total allowance:	$138	$149	$160	$171	$182	$193	$204	$216

Bankruptcy Allowable Living Expenses – National Standards
(See 11 U.S.C. § 707(b)(2)(A)(ii)(I))

Food & Clothing (Apparel & services)*	$93	$102	$111	$119	$131	$139	$150	$163
5% of Food & Clothing	5	5	6	6	7	7	8	8

* This total may differ from the combination of the two amounts on the table above due to rounding.

Table 11: IRS Allowable Expenses for Bankruptcy

These tables do not specify the amount of income that is allowed for religious donations. Whether one is filing bankruptcy protection under Chapters 7 or 13, they are allowed to donate up to 15 percent of their income to religious institutions and the amount must be counted in the calculation of one's monthly expenses. This amount may lower one's income such that one who would otherwise fail the means test and be required to file for protection under Chapter 13 could then file for protection under Chapter 7.

Failing both the first and second test, debtors may still qualify for bankruptcy protection under Chapter 7 if they are able to meet the third and final test.

The third test determines whether one's excess monthly income is greater than $100 for the next 60 months. If the $100 amount is available over the next five years and the total amount is enough to pay at least 25 percent of one's unsecured debts, they will not be able to file for bankruptcy protection under Chapter 7, though they may be able to file under Chapter 13.

QUALIFYING FOR PROTECTION UNDER CHAPTER 13

The new requirements to restrict bankruptcy filings under Chapter 7 are most likely to lead to more filings under Chapter 13. Bankruptcy protection under Chapter 13 has the same requirements for credit counseling and proof of income. If the means test requires filing under Chapter 13 and one's income is above the median for the state of residence, all disposable income must be used to pay off debts. One's disposable income is calculated as income minus allowable expenses defined by the IRS in Table 11. All disposable income must be paid to a trustee of the bankruptcy court who will then distribute it to creditors for the next five years unless the bankrupt individual can prove to the court that he or she is capable of paying off all debts in full in less than five years.

If the means test requires filing for bankruptcy protection under Chapter 13, but one's income is below the median income for the state of residence, all disposable income must be used to pay off debts. However, the period for repayment may be reduced from five years to three years.

THE DECISION TO FILE BANKRUPTCY

The decision to file bankruptcy will have an effect on certain life events for the next 10 or more years. The decision will affect one's finances, credit report, and self-image. Bankruptcy filings become part of public records that are accessible by creditors, employers, and other business entities. Bankruptcy information that is reported on one's credit report will have a negative and long lasting impact on one's credit score for up to 10 years. Bankruptcy is also considered a negative character attribute and others may view one who has filed bankruptcy as immoral, irresponsible, or just a bad person. Even so, bankruptcy may be the only alternative to relieving one's financial obligations after suffering a serious setback. Most often, the final decision to file bankruptcy is based on monetary needs, regardless of credit, credit scoring, or images. There are several consequences and options that one should take into consideration before making a final decision to file bankruptcy.

They include the following:

- **Ensure that a bankruptcy will have the effect of solving the financial situation.**

If one's financial hardship is due to overspending or using credit to supplement one's income, bankruptcy will not correct these types of behaviors. Bankruptcy may act as a temporarily band-aid to financial problems by relieving an individual of the obligation to pay acquired debts, but it will not change the spending habits that are responsible to create such debt.

- **Examine how bankruptcy will affect future priorities and goals.**

While a bankruptcy will remain on one's credit report for up to 10 years, the consequences of filing bankruptcy may extend far beyond the 10 year period. A lost job opportunity, for example, may affect one's career goals indefinitely.

- **Consider long-term consequences.**

It may be a mistake to base the decision to file bankruptcy solely on immediate circumstances, as is common. Consumers need to consider long-term life events, such as buying a home, renting a home, applying for a job, seeking a promotion, getting married, or getting a divorce. One way to examine how bankruptcy will affect future goals is to envision life in the next five years. Then assess how bankruptcy will affect your ability to reach your goals.

- **Explore other ways of reducing debt.**

It may be possible to increase one's income with a promotion or second job. However, consumers must be careful to ensure that an additional job is a real possibility. Employers, like creditors, examine credit reports and other specialty consumer reports when determining whether to hire or promote employees. If a credit report is already ruined, consumers may have a hard time gaining employment or a promotion. Even if one does, it may be short lived. It is possible that an employer will hire or promote an employee before running credit checks and other checks of consumer reports. That employee may then find that he or she is rejected, usually under the auspices of something other than bad credit, during the probationary period of the employment or promotion.

- **Get both professional legal and non-legal opinions as to whether to file bankruptcy.**

The new provisions of the BAPCPA require credit counseling within the six month period before filing bankruptcy, so that a non-legal professional opinion is required and may be acquired from a credit counselor. This non-legal professional is capable of advising on options, providing an analysis of one's income and spending behavior, devising a workable plan of action, and providing the consumer with a written budget or spending plan. Consumers should also seek a professional and legal opinion from an attorney who specializes in bankruptcies. This professional will also be capable of providing advice on options such as settlements. Bankruptcy attorneys will determine whether one's financial situation qualifies for bankruptcy and for which chapter of the bankruptcy code they qualify. They may also be willing to discuss the benefit or consequence of self-representation. Some courts are lenient in dealing with individuals who represent themselves; others are not so lenient.

- **Communicate with creditors and others.**

Consumers may want to communicate with creditors about an alternative repayment plan that had not been proposed or discussed before. Consumers are also encouraged to communicate with trusted friends and associates to gain a different perspective but to avoid conversations with persons who are owed money, persons who owe them money, dependents, and others persons who will be affected by a bankruptcy decision.

Opting Out, the Voluntary Dismissal

If, after filing for bankruptcy protection, an individual decides not to pursue it, the individual may request the court to dismiss the bankruptcy case voluntarily so long as the request comes before the discharge of the bankruptcy. One's credit file will continue to show a bankruptcy for the seven to ten years as required, and their credit score will continue to be lowered by the bankruptcy for the seven to ten-year period. The credit-reporting agency, however, must also indicate that the bankruptcy was dismissed.

Filing, Opting Out, and then Re-filing

Bankruptcy laws include provisions for individuals who file for bankruptcy protection, then opt out by requesting and receiving a voluntary dismissal of bankruptcy, then re-file for bankruptcy protection. These events must occur within a one year period. When one initially files for bankruptcy protection, the courts will enact an automatic stay (suspension) of collection activities by creditors included in the bankruptcy. The length of the stay may vary, dependent upon the type of debt or the action being stayed. In general, the length of a stay is from the time the paperwork is filed with the courts until the discharge of debts of the bankruptcy. After opting out of the bankruptcy and then re-filing for bankruptcy protection, an automatic stay is enacted, but only for 30 days. This means that the individual must complete all required paperwork, counseling, and testing within the 30 day window of opportunity or else the stay is lifted and collection activities may continue.

If an individual chooses to opt out of bankruptcy protection for a second time and then re-file for bankruptcy protection a third time within a one year period, no automatic stay is enacted. However, the court may specifically order a stay on behalf of the individual.

Once debts are discharged under either a Chapter 7 or Chapter 13 bankruptcy, an individual may not file for bankruptcy protection for an established number of years. If one files for Chapter 7 bankruptcy protection and has debts discharged, that person may not file for bankruptcy protection under Chapter 7 for the next eight years or under Chapter 13 for the next 6 years. If one files for protection under Chapter 13 and receives a discharge of debts, that person may not file for protection under Chapter 13 for the next two years or protection under Chapter 7 for the next four years.

LIFE AFTER BANKRUPTCY

Bankruptcy may eliminate debt collectors, the fees and penalty rates assessed against default payments, threats of legal action, and legal actions. However, there are some severe consequences to filing bankruptcy. One must begin to rebuild credit, use credit carefully, and provide a good explanation for the bankruptcy in their credit file.

Obtaining Credit

Bankruptcies are included on one's credit report in the public records section. This mark remains on a credit report for at least 10 years. It may cause one's credit score to decrease by as much as 100 points. Lenders and creditors may increase interest rates or decline future credit because of the bankruptcy and the resulting low credit score. However, there are other lenders who will extend credit to individuals who have filed bankruptcy. These lenders understand that the consumer cannot file bankruptcy again for eight years and they are likely to be paid and at the highest possible interest rates. Some of these types of lenders are known to take advantage of the situation and engage bankrupt consumers into signing contractual agreements that allow for excessive interest rates and penalties. They also tend to be more inconsiderate in their collection activities. Consumers must be sure to seek reputable lenders following a bankruptcy.

The better one's credit score prior to filing bankruptcy, the more their credit score will drop due to a bankruptcy. If one had bad credit before filing for bankruptcy, the bankruptcy will not cause their credit score to drop that much. The same components of a credit file that impact credit score calculations are impacted by a bankruptcy.

- **Payment History**. More than half of all bankruptcies are filed with no prior instances of delinquency. That means half of bankruptcies are filed with prior delinquencies. The more problems that existed prior to bankruptcy, the lower one's credit score will be.

- **Amounts Owed**. A bankruptcy causes most or all accounts to be closed by the person filing for protection or the lender who issued the account. The amount of available credit on these accounts will be $0, reducing one's credit score.

- **Length of Credit History**. The history of all accounts included in the bankruptcy will be shortened by the bankruptcy and damage one's credit score.

- **Types of Credit**. It is likely that only secured debts such as mortgages will be left after bankruptcy, and unsecured debts such as credit cards will be closed. This action limits the variety of accounts used to increase one's credit score.

- **New Requests for Credit**. New applications for credit may be necessary in an attempt to re-establish a credit history after bankruptcy. The more inquiries included in one's credit file, the lower the credit score.

Companies that receive notice that an individual has filed for bankruptcy protection will use make use of the notices to develop mailing lists for solicitation and telemarketing. These types of companies attempt to take advantage of the personal and financial vulnerabilities of individuals who have credit problems due to a bankruptcy. They are most likely to advertise the ability to provide a new start by offering high-cost credit products with exorbitant terms and conditions embedded in fine print.

Consumers may opt out of solicitations by credit agency and direct marketing mailing programs that make pre-approved offers for credit products. Consumers may remove their names and addresses from mailing lists obtained from the major credit reporting agencies by visiting the Web site, **www.optoutprescreen.com**, or calling 1-888-567-8688. Consumers may opt out of mailing lists compiled by direct marketing companies that subscribe to the Direct Marketing Association by contacting the association as follows:

Mail Service Listings	Phone Service Listings
Direct Marketing Association	Direct Marketing Association
Mail Preference Service	Telephone Preference Service
P.O. Box 643	P.O. Box 1559
Carmel, New York 10512	Carmel, New York 10512

The request to opt out of mailing and phone lists should include one's name, current address, and phone number (in the case of phone lists). Consumers may also prevent unsolicited calls from telemarketers by registering to have their name and phone number placed on the Federal Trade Commission (FTC) Do Not Call Registry by visiting the Web site at **www.donotcall.gov.**

Individuals should prepare a statement that describes valid reasons for seeking bankruptcy protection. Creditors and business entities may be willing to do business with individuals who provide valid reasons for their bankruptcy. This statement is not a part of the 100 word written statement that consumers are allowed to add to their credit files. This is a verbal statement that consumers should make to creditors or other business entities that will pull their credit report before completing business and credit transactions. Consumers are encouraged to provide this verbal reasoning before the creditor or business entity pulls a credit report to make sure that they will actually be pulling the credit report. In other words, unless asked, do not open Pandora's box. The statement should be positive, short, and rehearsed. It is best if the bankruptcy is attributable to a single traumatic event, such as divorce or illness. It would be even better if the language of the statement indicates a situation over which one had no control. It should indicate that all possible avenues were taken in an attempt to meet financial obligations and end with some words of wisdom or lessons learned. The statement should not be an explanation of one's attempt to pay debts or deal with debt collectors. A statement should be devised as follows:

When you view my credit report, you will notice that I filed for bankruptcy. I'm not proud of this, but I had no choice. Because of a complicated divorce, I was left with thousands of dollars worth of debt. I am now in a position to manage my own debts. It was a painful lesson to learn, but I am ready to move forward.

RENTING

Landlords and property management companies have permissible purpose in obtaining credit reports on individuals who make application to rent homes, apartments, or other types of rental property. A bankruptcy may be grounds to refuse rental, require a co-signer, or increase any required deposits on the rental property.

INSURANCE

Insurance companies have a permissible purpose for obtaining credit reports on individuals who seek insurance. In states that allow insurance companies to factor in credit scores in establishing insurance premiums, a bankruptcy becomes cause for charging consumers higher insurance premiums. Home and vehicle insurers are most likely to use credit reports. Bankruptcies are also cause for rate increases for insured parties, even if they have no loss or claims against the insurer.

EMPLOYMENT

Legally one cannot be denied employment because of a bankruptcy so employers will make use of their permissible purpose in acquiring a credit score and deny bankrupt individuals employment without actually asking about or mentioning the bankruptcy, thus protecting themselves from any legal actions. A bankruptcy may also prevent the issuance of certain licenses and security clearances.

SELF IMAGE

Most people wrap the view of themselves in their financial persona. A bankruptcy may be responsible for causing internal conflict for some individuals. Some persons have gone so far as to resort to suicide and suicide attempts in an effort to stop the inner turmoil.

Obtaining a Mortgage

Bad credit or a bankruptcy may not prevent consumers from obtaining a mortgage. If a consumer is able to convince the mortgage lender that the unusual financial circumstances that led to bankruptcy, such as a divorce or illness, have been resolved and their finances are back in order, the consumer will have a better chance of obtaining a mortgage. Further, if the bankruptcy has been discharged for at least four years and the consumer has reestablished credit, the chances of obtaining a mortgage are increased. If the consumer is seeking an FHA loan, most lenders will require that the bankruptcy be discharged for at least two years and that credit has been reestablished. Consumers, who file bankruptcy under Chapter 13 may make application for a mortgage after completing at least one year of payments under their repayment plan and receive approval from a trustee of the bankruptcy court to add a mortgage to debts. Consumers are advised to do the following:

Work with a mortgage broker to acquire a mortgage. Most brokers work with several different lenders and are capable of "selling" mortgage applications to more flexible lenders.

Settle for a lower grade mortgage. Mortgages that fall into the guidelines established by mortgage investors, such as Fannie Mae and Freddie Mac are considered "A" quality loans. Other mortgages fall into "B", "C," and "D" quality and may be more achievable. These mortgage loans usually cost more. They offer higher interest rates, points, and, in most instances, a higher down payment. Consumers, who are capable of obtaining a lower grade mortgage and make timely payments on their account may refinance for better rates after negative information is removed from their credit files.

Obtain a mortgage that is carried back. A mortgage is carried back when a homeowner holds no mortgage against a property and sells the property, allowing the buyer to make payments, including interest, directly to the homeowner instead of a bank. This type of arrangement requires the services of a competent real estate attorney, but it is perfectly legal.

DEBT MANAGEMENT VERSUS BANKRUPTCY

The BAPCPA requires that persons seeking bankruptcy protection engage in credit counseling before filing bankruptcy. After filing for protection, but before the discharge from the bankruptcy, individuals are required to complete a course in financial management. These requirements are intended to provide bankrupt individuals with an unbiased assessment of their financial situation and an opportunity to learn to handle their finances and debt better.

One of the primary benefits of credit counseling is that it will help individuals with establishing a debt management plan, a voluntary arrangement set up with creditors through a credit counseling agency. Creditors are not required to accept the terms of any debt management plan established by the credit counseling agency. However, most creditors welcome a debt management plan because it indicates that the debt will be paid, even if not necessarily as specified by the terms of the original agreement. The alternative for creditors would be to reject the debt management plan and have the consumer file for bankruptcy. Bankruptcy signifies that the creditor may never be paid in full or in part. The disadvantage to creditors is that a consumer may opt out of a debt management plan at any given time and still file for bankruptcy protection.

A debt management plan offers advantages over filing bankruptcy because it is less restrictive and least likely to damage one's credit score. Debt management is more advantageous than Chapter 13 bankruptcy protection. The consumer will have a less restrictive payment plan and may later opt to file for bankruptcy if the debt management plan does not work in the consumer's favor.

Payment to Creditors

A debt management plan allows creditors to collect payments in addition to finance charges. However, the finance charge may be reduced to a rate that is more affordable to the consumer. Under Chapter 7 bankruptcy protection, most debts are liquidated and creditors might not receive any payment. The payment may amount to what was originally owed. The creditor cannot apply interest to the payment amounts. Under Chapter 13 protection, the creditor loses the difference between what is ultimately paid and what was to be paid originally.

Disposable Income

Under a debt management plan, any disposable income goes into a savings plan for emergencies. Disposable income is the remaining income after paying living expenses and creditors. Under Chapter 13 bankruptcy, all of one's disposable income is required to be paid to creditors, and IRS guidelines are used to determine the amount of one's income that may be used for living expenses.

Credit Scores

Accounts discharged in bankruptcy are recorded in one's credit file in the payment history section and may remain there for up to 10 years. A bankruptcy is considered a negative mark with a negative impact on one's credit score. Debt management plans, on the other hand, are established through credit counseling, and many creditors do not report this information to credit reporting agencies. Other creditors do report it as a description of the included accounts, not as payment history entries like those accounts included in bankruptcy. Unlike account descriptions, payment history entries are used in calculating credit scores. A credit report may show an account type as credit counseling, but the payment history may read "paid as agreed" or "30 days late." An account discharged in bankruptcy will be recorded in both the public records section and payment history section of a credit report. If the account was discharged under Chapter 7 of the bankruptcy code, the account entry will read, "Discharged under Chapter 7 Bankruptcy." A credit counseling notation in a credit file is perceived as a neutral entry, which means it will not affect credit score calculations.

Any credit counseling account descriptions included in one's credit file will remain there until the account is paid or the debt management plan is discontinued. At such time, the description is removed. It does not remain in one's credit file for seven to ten years, as do accounts included in bankruptcy.

CHAPTER

9

MAINTAINING GOOD CREDIT

A good credit rating improves one's credit score and assists with obtaining the most favorable interest rates on purchases. Credit reports should be checked regularly and at least three months before making a major purchase. Some salespersons, particularly those who are responsible for arranging financing for large purchases such as homes, cars, or boats, and those who receive a commission, may try to convince an individual that he or she is a credit risk when in fact they have good credit. These salespersons use this tactic in an attempt to sell products at higher interest rates than are required. Regular checks should be made every six to twelve months for inaccuracies as well as symptoms of identity theft. In addition to checking credit reports regularly, consumers should reduce their debts, maintain a healthy balance of credit types, pay their bills on time, keep credit card balances below 35 percent of the credit limit and quickly correct any negative entries on their credit reports to maintain good credit.

MAINTAIN A HEALTHY BALANCE OF CREDIT

A mix of credit types that includes credit cards, retail accounts, mortgages, finance accounts, and installment loans creates a healthy balance of credit that will improve one's credit score. The mix of credit types indicates that a consumer is capable of handling multiple types of repayment obligations. Credit card payments, for example, require a minimum payment each month; installment loans require a fixed payment each month. Consumers must be careful not to include too many accounts to avoid high-interest and high-risk lenders, such as with most payday loans, and not open too many new accounts at one time. Multiple inquiries and multiple new accounts may have a negative effect on one's credit score. New accounts should be acquired over time. The mix of credit is not so important in calculating a credit score that one needs to have all types of credit, but when multiple credit accounts are held, it is best that they are composed of a mix of credit types. At least one type of credit should be an installment loan because they help one's credit score the most. Other types of credit should be used to pay for things that one normally buys and the consumer should then pay the balance in full.

Non-Installment Credit

Non-installment credit is a type of consumer credit where the account balance must be paid in full each month. Consumers are not allowed to carry a balance. It is the simplest form of a credit card, which allows one to make unplanned purchases when cash is not readily available. Non-installment credit is offered as a convenience to the cardholder and a benefit to merchants.

Installment, Closed-End Credit

Installment, closed-end credit allows for the purchase of items with credit extended for the amount of the purchase. This type of credit is usually offered by department, furniture, electronics, and appliance stores. In some special cases, the amount of the purchase is loaned to the consumer and the consumer is given a deadline when the first payment is due or a deadline before any interest is applied to the loan amount. Merchants who advertise loans as interest-free for six months or no payment for six months are advertising installment, closed-end credit loans.

Revolving, Open-End Credit

Revolving, open-end credit is extended for traditional credit cards. Consumers are granted a credit amount that may be used at will. Consumers have the option of paying the bill in full each month or paying the required minimum amount and carrying the balance forward to the next month.

Credit Cards

Until the passage of the federal Fair Credit and Charge Card Disclosure Act of 1989, creditors would issue credit cards without disclosing the interest rate and other fees associated with the card until the consumer actually accepted and received the card. This act requires that creditors disclose the terms of a credit card before the consumer makes application for the card and that the cost of the card is displayed in an easy-to-read box format on most applications and solicitations. The box format, also termed the Schumer Box, is so named because it was Senator Charles Schumer of New York who pushed this consumer protection legislation through Congress.

The major types of credit cards include the following:

VISA AND MASTERCARD

Visa and MasterCard are the most popular types of bank credit cards offered at a variety of prices with a variety of perks. Visa and MasterCard themselves do not issue credit cards. They are large financial institutions that provide the systems and support to thousands of banks across the country in issuing credit cards. As such, these banks act as franchises to the Visa and MasterCard systems. Banks and other financial institutions, such as credit unions and savings banks, must abide by basic rules established by Visa and MasterCard, but the issuing financial institutions are free to establish their own credit standards, limits, prices, and other offerings to its cardholders. The issuing banks also determine which customers should get cards. One may be denied a card at one bank and be accepted by another.

Visa and MasterCard are similar in terms of the conveniences they offer and the buying power they afford cardholders. It is commonplace for consumers to hold one or more of each type of card. Visa and MasterCard also offer the convenience of being accepted by most merchants around the globe.

DISCOVER CARD

A subsidiary of Morgan Stanley Dean Witter and Co., Discover Financial Services offers the Discover card, a bank credit card that was introduced as a competitor to MasterCard and Visa with its offering of a 1 percent cash back rebate on purchases made with the card. Millions of consumers hold Discover Cards, which are accepted by many merchants in the U.S. but it has no international acceptance. Discover Cards are issued as Classic, Gold, Platinum and they also issue an Affinity card.

AMERICAN EXPRESS

American Express entered the market purely as a charge card that required consumers to pay the balance for purchases in full each month. Charge cards still dominate American Express cards, but they have added credit cards to their products for customers. An American Express charge card is issued as a personal card (Green) or a Gold card. American Express credit cards are offered as Blue, Optima and Optima Platinum. The Blue card includes a SmartChip that provides its customers with an extra level of security when shopping online.

American Express is best known for having no preset spending limit, implying that customers are allowed to charge as much as they want on the card. However, the reality of American Express is their cards offer flexibility in allowing customers to make purchases, but most customers do not really know how much they are allowed to charge. American Express uses software to track their customer's spending behavior, and if a customer appears to be spending too much, a representative may contact the customer to inquire about the spending behavior. American Express may decline the customer's purchase or they may freeze the card if they believe the customer is not going to be capable of paying the bill. The exact methodology used in determining an amount that is considered too much for any one customer is unknown.

American Express, through its advertisements, which include famous persons and celebrities, has established itself as a prestigious card. Many people, both young and old, are attracted to the prestige associated with the card. American Express also advertises itself as providing superior customer service, which is above and beyond that offered by other card companies. These, along with the many perks that are also offered by the company, tend to attract and retain customers.

DEPARTMENT STORE CARDS

Department store cards are easy to acquire, but they are one of the most expensive types of credit cards. Though many department store cards have no annual fee associated with them, they often charge astronomical interest rates if purchases are not paid in full each month. Interest rates generally range between 18 and 26 percent. The biggest advantage to department store cards is that cardholders are privy to advance notice of special sales and discounts. Cardholders are also invited to private sales and they are offered special discounts on merchandise.

GASOLINE CARDS

Gasoline cards differ from co-branded cards offered by gas companies. Co-branded cards are Visa and MasterCard credit cards with a gas company's name on the card. Gasoline cards usually require that balances for purchases be paid in full each month with the exception of higher ticket items. Such items may include car repairs, travel, and tires. These items may be purchased with revolving lines of credit, which may be carried forward from month to month. As with department store cards, the interest rate on these revolving lines of credit is usually high. Gasoline cards are relatively easy to acquire. The benefit to gasoline cards is that cardholders are offered perks, such as travel club memberships, emergency road assistance, and credit card registrations.

SPECIALTY CREDIT CARDS

Gold Cards

Gold cards are considered prestigious since they are only offered to exceptional customers, generally those who make at least $35,000 per year and have a good credit rating. The prestige of Gold cards has declined since American Express is not the only card issuer to offer Gold cards, and millions of Gold cards are now in circulation. Gold cards usually offer higher credit limits, in the range of $5,000 to many thousands of dollars. In contrast, standard credit cards offer lines of credit in the range of $2,000 to $3,000. However, many standard credit cards have competitively extended credit limits to match those of gold cards. Gold cards offer many perks that standard credit cards do not offer. Perks may include such things as emergency medical services, legal services when cardholders are traveling, vehicle collision coverage for rental cars, purchase protection plans, and extended warranties.

Affinity Cards

Affinity cards are most often associated with charities and associations. Affinity credit cards carry the logo or name of the sponsoring group and usually advertise to donate a portion of each purchase or a part of the annual fee to the sponsoring group. Affinity cards are often more expensive than other credit cards, requiring high interest rates and a standard annual fee of about $20. Some affinity card issuers will waive the annual fee for the first six months or first year. The charitable donation is not tax deductible to the cardholder, and the card issuer will not disclose the amount donated to charitable organizations because that information is proprietary. Many affinity cards are associated with groups for which no real sponsor exits. Banks that issue affinity cards for groups, such as mystery book lovers and golfers, sponsor themselves and any donation is paid back to them.

Debit Cards

Debit cards are not credit cards, though many look like Visa and MasterCard credit cards. Debit cards are used to access money in one's brokerage, checking, or savings account rather than a line of credit. Cardholders are not entitled to use of the bank's money until it is paid at the end of the month as with credit cards. Debit card use is not reported to credit reporting agencies and will have no effect in helping to repair or build credit. Debit cards may be used for purchases and ATM transactions. With the exception of rental car agencies, merchants who accept Visa and MasterCard credit cards must also accept debit cards that carry the Visa and MasterCard logo. Some rental car agencies will not accept debit cards. Some debit cards incur fees for their use from the debit card issuer as well as merchants .The debit card agreement should specify any fees associated with use of the card. Most debit cards limit the amount of cash that may be withdrawn from accounts each day and any holds on a cardholder's account may prevent access to cash in the account. Such holds are commonplace for hotels and rental car agencies. Some debit card issuers offer perks, such as rebates and frequent flyer miles. ATM cards are a type of debit card that only lets cardholders access their accounts from ATM machines. ATM cards may not be used for purchases. Some gasoline cards also offer a debit feature that allows gas purchases to be drawn directly from one's account. Debit cards work either online or offline.

Online transactions require a cardholder to use a PIN number for ATM transactions and purchases. The amount of an online transaction is immediately applied to the cardholder's account. Online transactions are routed through one of many networks that are responsible for processing these types of transactions. The particular network is transparent to the cardholder and usually becomes of interest only when there is a problem with a transaction. Debit cards are not included in the Fair Credit Billing Act. As such, cardholders are not allowed to withhold payment in the case of disputes. Cardholders must deal directly with the merchant, which can become a big problem if the merchant is not legitimate. The federal Electronic Funds Transfer Act governs debit cards. If a debit card is lost or stolen, the cardholder's liability is $50, but only if the loss or theft is reported to the card issuer within two business days. Waiting longer to report the loss or theft of a debit card increases the cardholder's liability to an unlimited amount. However, both Visa and MasterCard have policies to protect cardholders from unlimited liability if their debit card is used fraudulently. Some debit card issuers place a limit on the number of transactions that may be made within a specified time, such as a month, before fees are assessed against each transaction. Merchants prefer to engage in online transactions because they are cheaper than offline transactions.

Offline transactions do not require the use of a PIN number. Transactions are carried out just as if the cardholder were writing a check or using a credit card. A debit card is swiped at the cash register terminal and the purchase is treated as a credit card purchase. The amount of the purchase is applied to the cardholder's account within a period of one to three days, the time that checks usually require to clear. Persons who have a bank account should be capable of getting a debit card, but if their credit or checking history is bad, they may not be allowed to make offline purchases. Debit card issuers prefer offline transactions because they profit from the merchant fee that is paid for transactions.

Home Equity Loans

Home equity loans require borrowers to use the equity in their homes as collateral for loans. Doing so helps to reduce the interest rate on the loan. However, those who default on their home equity loans risk losing the home that secures the loan. There are two types of home equity loans: a second mortgage and a home equity line of credit. A second mortgage is an installment loan for a fixed amount of money. The entire amount of the loan is borrowed at once and paid with regular monthly payments. A home equity line of credit requires that the borrower be approved for a line of credit for a certain amount. The borrower may then borrow amounts up to the limit of the line of credit. A home equity line of credit is a sort of revolving line of credit since the borrower may borrow money against the loan on an as-needed basis and the monthly payment amount is based on the account balance.

Generally, a home equity loan may be acquired for 50 to 80 percent of the value of the home, minus any existing mortgage amount. Some subprime lenders offer home equity loans for as much as 100 percent to 125 percent of the value of the home. Having a home equity loan that exceeds the value of the home presents a problem if the borrower decides to sell the home or the value of the home depreciates. The borrower becomes upside down in the loan, which means the debt against the home is more than the home is worth. If the borrower sells the home for less than its assessed value, the borrower will have to pay the difference between the outstanding balance of the home equity loan and the sale price of the property.

A home equity loan offers tax advantages, making it a great tool for consolidating debts that offer no tax advantages, such as vehicle loans and credit cards. Borrowers who itemize deductions on their tax returns may deduct the interest on home equity loans up to the value of the home or up to a cap of $100,000. Any portion of the loan that exceeds the value of the home or exceeds the cap is not tax deductible. If a home equity loan is used to pay for educational or medical expenses, the full amount of interest is tax deductible, regardless of the amount.

The interest on a home equity loan is often lower than the interest on other types of consumer loans. Most home equity lines of credit are offered at variable interest rates. Variable interest rates change with the economy and the borrower must decide whether such a loan is cost effective should interest rates rise. Some home equity loans offer an interest-only payment method. This method of payment allows for lower payments since the borrower is only paying the interest that incurs on the loan rather than paying down the principal balance of the loan. Borrowers who intend to sell property quickly and wish to reduce the payment to a minimum in the process usually use the interest-only payment method. This payment method may also be useful during hard economic times. The low payment amounts may be responsible for keeping the borrower from facing a financial crisis or bankruptcy. As part of their marketing scheme, some home equity lenders may offer teaser, or introductory rates, for their loans. These rates are usually low to attract customers, but the introductory rate only applies for a short time, maybe six months or a year. After the introductory rate has expired, the borrower may be required to pay an expectantly high interest rate. Consumers should rate shop by comparing the annual percentage rates that will be applied outside the introductory period.

Some home equity loans require no fees and closing costs, while others have fees and closing costs that may cost thousands of dollars. Closing costs include such things as appraisal fees, title search fees, title insurance, or recording fees. Consumers must be sure to request that lenders disclose all applicable fees before entering a contractual agreement. Some home equity loans may require that a loan origination fee be paid in advance of receiving the loan. Some lenders assess a loan origination fee to cover the cost of preparing, packaging, and processing a loan. This fee is equivalent to one point, which is assessed as 1 percent of the loan amount.

Some lenders report the account history of home equity loans to credit reporting agencies; others do not. If a home equity loan appears on one's credit report, it may be responsible for giving the borrower a large available line of credit, even when the borrower does not make use of the entire line of credit. As such, a home equity loan may be responsible for causing other creditors to reject applications for credit based on the large available line of credit.

Personal Loans

Personal loans are unsecured loans which are offered by most banks. Personal loans may be acquired in the range of thousands of dollars. Interest rates on personal loans may be lower than interest rates on most credit cards, but also higher than the interest rate of most low-rate credit cards. Consumers should attempt to acquire a personal loan with the bank with which they hold their savings and checking accounts. Most banks offer easier approval criteria and better terms to their regular customers. Personal loans may be used to consolidate existing high-rate credit accounts. Customers with too much existing credit or too much available credit may be considered a poor risk for personal loans since they may easily charge up to their available limits at any time.

Joint Credit

Joint credit is acquired by more than one person. Each person provides signature to a contractual agreement to make sufficient and timely payments on the credit account. The history of this joint account is included in the credit file of each person who is party to the contractual agreement. Joint debt acquired through marriage is defined as equally owned by both spouses. In community property states, both spouses equally own debts of the other spouse. With the exception of a gift or inheritance, both debt and property acquired during a marriage is considered community property. There are nine community property states in the United States.

MANAGE CREDIT ACCOUNTS

To manage credit accounts properly, one must be aware of his or her debt and know how any future extensions of credit may affect that debt. Lines of credit should be managed so that they appear on the consumer's credit report, provide the lowest interest rates attainable, and require low or no annual fees. The consumer must be aware of the terms of any credit agreement, particularly those provided for such services as cell phones and online services. These types of agreements require payments for the term of the agreement, which may be months or years. Even when the service is no longer used, payments may still be required, or a service fee may be required for early termination of the agreement.

Credit debt should be managed by paying down the debt. Doing so not only reduces the interest that is charged for credit, but it improves one's credit score. A credit score is higher if a consumer has some small debts rather than no debt or large debts. Consumers should keep track of the credit limits and debt for all credit accounts, particularly revolving accounts. If consumers are using more than 50 percent of the available credit limit, they should either pay down the debt or increase the credit limit to reduce their debt-to-credit ratio.

Managing Credit Card Debt

Credit cards can be the most expensive or the cheapest form of consumer loans, depending on the offering stipulated in the fine print of the credit card agreement. Fair priced credit cards are available, but they are often harder to find and harder to qualify for. There are five basic elements to a credit card. They include finance charges, annual fees, grace periods, penalty fees, and balance calculation methods. A typical disclosure table for a credit card includes all of these elements as follows:

Credit Card Disclosure Table	
Finance Charge for Purchases	19.8% APR, with a minimum of $.50
Finance Charge for Cash Advances	25%
Transaction Fee for Cash Advances	2% with a minimum of $2
Annual Fee	$25 per year
Grace Period	25 days
Penalty Fees	Late payment: $10
Balance Calculation Method	Average daily balance, including new purchases

FINANCE CHARGES

The finance charge, also called interest, is the commission that consumers pay to creditors for lending them money. For most credit cards, if the balance is not paid in full each month, a finance charge is applied to the balance. It is estimated that between one-third and one-half of all cardholders fail to pay the balance on credit cards in full. Finance charges are documented on credit card statements as a monthly periodic rate and also as an annual percentage rate (APR). An APR of 19.8 percent indicates the amount of interest that will be applied over a one year period. When the 19.8 percent APR is divided by 12 months, a monthly periodic rate of 1.65 percent is obtained. The monthly periodic rate seems minimal, but that percentage rate is applied to the entire balance. A monthly period rate of 1.65 percent applied to a $1,000 balance amounts to $17 per month (.0165*1000) and more than $200 per year. On the other hand, a monthly periodic rate of 1.65 percent applied to a balance of $5,000 amounts to $83 per month (.0165 x 5000) and close to $1,000 per year.

ANNUAL FEES

Some credit cards have an annual fee that must be paid on a yearly basis for the use of the card. Annual fees may range from $0 to $100, but the average annual fee charged to consumers is $20. Many credit card companies do not charge an annual fee but rely upon the interest paid on account balances by cardholders who fail to pay the entire balance each month to generate a profit. In addition to interest payments, credit card companies receive what is termed a merchant discount fee from merchants. A merchant discount fee is a percentage of purchases paid to the credit card company for the privilege of being able to accept their particular card. Merchant discount fees may range from 1.5 percent to 4 percent of the purchase amount. The credit card issuer pays a small portion of the merchant discount fee.

GRACE PERIODS

Grace periods are the time from the date when payment is due and the closing date of the billing cycle. If payment is made during this time in full, no interest is applied to the balance of accounts. Grace periods are only beneficial if payment is made in full at the end of the billing cycle. If partial payment of a balance is made during the grace period, interest is still applied to the account balance. In most instances, making a partial payment during the grace period only avoids having any additional late charges applied to the account balance. When a credit card offers a grace period, the credit card statement will usually read something to the effect of "Pay this amount to avoid further finance charges...." When a credit card does not offer a grace period, interest will be applied to the account balance regardless of whether the balance is paid in full or not. The credit card statement will indicate the total amount of payment, including interest, to be paid.

PENALTY FEES

Credit card companies may assess penalties against credit card accounts for particular transactions such as when payments are made late, when cardholders' balances extend over-the-limit, or when payment is made with a check that bounces. Penalty fees are supposed to penalize cardholders who fail to pay their accounts as agreed. The fees can be quite expensive and rarely do credit card companies limit the amount assessed to the actual cost of processing the particular transaction. Besides, the interest that is applied to account balances is supposed to cover the cost of transactions and also provide the company with a reasonable profit. Some credit card issuers further increase their profits by applying penalty fees to the account balance and then applying interest to both the balance and the penalty amount.

Cash Advances

Cash advances usually incur interest from the date that the advance was made, regardless of whether payment is made in full at the end of the billing cycle. Most credit card issuers charge more interest for cash advances than they do for purchases. In addition, a one time fee for cash advances is usually applied just for the privilege of making the cash advance. This cash advance fee may range from 2 percent to 4 percent of the amount of cash advanced, but may be capped at $25 to $50. The fine print of the cardholder's agreement will disclose the terms and conditions of cash advances.

Some credit card issuers may advertise that they charge a cash advance fee rather than applying interest to the cash advance right away. In most instances, the cash advance fee is far more than the interest that would be applied to the balance of the cash advance. Further, if the balance of the account is not paid in full by the due date, interest is still applied to the account balance.

Other Transaction Fees

Transaction fees are charged just for the privilege of using certain credit cards. A typical transaction fee is $.50 and it is applied each time the credit card is used. Though few credit card issuers charge transaction fess, when such a charge is applied to usage, the cardholder is not likely to know of the charge until it appears on a credit card statement. Consumers must read the fine print that accompanies credit card agreements to learn of such charges.

Late Fees

Late fees are assessed against account balances when payments are not made timely. Late fees may range from $10 to $35 and are usually assessed if payment is late by as little as one day or one minute. Most card issuers specify a due date as well as a time of day, such as 12 a.m., for which payment must be received before it is considered late. Also excessive late fees may be cause for some card issuers to raise interest rates for the cardholder.

Over-the-Limit Fees

Over-the-limit fees are assessed when cardholders exceed the limit of the account established by the card issuer. This fee may be assessed at $10 to $35, and interest is applied to the fee. Cardholders will usually be sent a notice from the card issuer requesting that they pay the amount that is over the limit immediately. In most cases, the over-the-limit fee is assessed each month that the cardholder remains over the limit. Over-the-limit fees indicate a great profit potential for the card issuers. Either the cardholder is carrying a high balance, which equates to many interest payments, or the cardholder has made many purchases within the billing cycle, which generates merchant discount fees for the card issuer.

BALANCE CALCULATION METHODS

The method that credit card issuers use to calculate finance charges and account balances plays an important role in determining the cost of a credit card. Credit cards are not like loans where a fixed amount is paid each month. Cardholders constantly borrow different amounts of money against their credit limits and pay back part or all of their account balance within a billing cycle. Balance calculation involves determining which balance to calculate interest on. Credit card issuers may use one of several methods of balance calculation. Some methods are more expensive to the consumer than others, and all are relatively complicated. Six of the most common balance calculation methods are as follows:

Adjusted Balance

Payments and credits made during the billing cycle are deducted from the account balance at the beginning of the billing cycle. If one's account balance is $100 at the beginning of the billing cycle and $90 was paid during the billing cycle, interest would be charged on the remaining $10 of the account balance. If charges of $100 were also made during the billing cycle, the balance at the beginning of the next billing cycle would be $110 plus the interest that is charged on the $10 remaining from the previous month.

Previous Balance

Interest is charged on the account balance at the beginning of the billing cycle. Payments and charges made during the billing cycle will not affect this interest but will be included in the account balance for the next month.

Average Daily Balance Excluding New Purchases

Payments and credits are deducted from the account balance at the beginning of the billing cycle for each day of the billing cycle. The total amount summed over all days in the billing cycle is then divided by the number of days in the billing cycle to arrive at an average daily balance. Interest is applied to the average daily balance. Purchases and credits made during the billing cycle have no effect on the account balance or interest applied to the account balance. These purchases will be used in the next month's balance calculation.

Average Daily Balance Including New Purchases

Payments and credits are deducted while purchases are added to the account balance at the beginning of the billing cycle, for each day of the billing cycle. The total amount summed over all days in the billing cycle is then divided by the number of days in the billing cycle to arrive at an average daily balance. Interest is applied to the average daily balance. Purchases made during the billing cycle raise the account balance as well as the interest applied to the account balance.

Two Cycle Average Daily Balance Excluding New Purchases

The account balance is calculated as the sum of two average daily balances, taken over two billing cycles. The first balance is calculated by deducting payments and credits from the outstanding balance at the start of the current billing cycle for each day of the billing cycle. The total amount summed over all days in the current billing cycle is then divided by the number of days in the current billing cycle to arrive at an average daily balance for the current billing cycle. The second balance is calculated in the same manner, except that it is calculated for the preceding billing cycle. Interest is applied to both the current month's balance and the previous month's balance. New purchases made in the previous month are added to the current month's starting balance. New purchases made in the current month have no affect on either of the balances used in the calculation or the interest applied to the balances.

Two Cycle Average Daily Balance Including New Purchases

The account balance is calculated as the sum of two average daily balances over two billing cycles. The first balance is calculated by adding purchases while deducting payments and credits from the outstanding balance at the start of the current billing cycle for each day of the billing cycle. The total amount summed over all days in the current billing cycle is then divided by the number of days in the billing cycle to arrive at an average daily balance for the current billing cycle. The second balance is calculated in the same manner, except that it is calculated for the preceding billing cycle. Interest is applied to both the current month's balance and the previous month's balance.

An ironic twist to the two cycle balance calculation methods is that there is no benefit to paying the balance in full if one is going to continue to use the card.

TYPES OF CREDIT CARD USERS

Credit users may be divided into three categories: true credit users, convenience users, and combination users. True credit users carry a balance from month to month and are likely to make only the minimum monthly payment or a partial payment each month. These users should seek credit cards with the lowest interest rates. For true credit users, annual fees are not so important since the cardholder is more likely to benefit from low interest rates than cheap annual fees. Grace periods are even less important since these users will not be capable of taking advantage of them. Grace periods are only beneficial to cardholders who pay their balance in full each month.

Convenience users make use of their credit cards, but pay the balance in full each month. These users should seek credit cards with low or no annual fee as well as interest free grace periods. If there is no grace period, this type of user will pay interest unnecessarily. Interest rates are less important for these users since the balance will be paid in full and no interest will be applied.

Combination users carry forward a balance about 50 percent of the time and pay the balance in full the rest of the time. These users should seek credit cards that offer a grace period, low interest rates, and low or no annual fees.

HOW TO SAVE ON CREDIT CARD USE

There are two methods of saving money on credit card use: save with existing cards or switch to another card. Consumers who hold credit cards with high interest rates or large annual fees should contact the card issuer and indicate to them that they wish to close their credit card account and acquire a card at a cheaper rate elsewhere. In response, some card issuers will waive or reduce the annual fee or offer a cheaper interest rate to retain good customers. Consumers with bad payment histories may not receive a better offer. If the initial contact does not result in a better offer, the consumer may request to speak with someone with higher authority. When consumers cannot acquire a better deal with existing card issuers, they should switch to another card.

Before closing out an account on an existing credit card, consumers should make application for a new card and get the new card in hand. After making application and receiving one card, the consumer may make application for another card. Consumers should not make application for more than one card at a time because card issuers may view this action as negative and deny an application. Once the consumer is sure to qualify for new cards, several options are available as follows:

Let the new card issuer transfer any account balances. Many card issuers will pay off cardholders' old account balances and transfer the balance to the new card account. Balance transfers, as they are called, only require that the cardholder sign a form specifying the accounts to be transferred. If the transfer is approved, the new and cheaper card issuer will take care of transfer. Balance transfers are also used as a marketing tool for card issuers wishing to acquire new customers. For some consumers, particularly those with good credit ratings, the offer may come in the mail.

Request convenience checks from the new card issuer. Convenience checks resemble personal checks except they are drawn against a credit card's line of credit. These checks may be used for purchases or anything of choice, including paying off other credit card balances. Consumers must be sure to read the fine print associated with convenience checks since most are billed at the interest rate applied to cash advances, which is usually much higher than the interest rate for purchases. Some card issuers, however, will bill convenience checks at the same rate as purchases, and for new customers, an introductory rate may apply. As with balance transfers, convenience checks are used as a marketing tool for some card issuers to attract new customers. For some consumers, the offer of convenience checks may be in the mail.

If a consumer is not able to obtain a balance transfer or convenience checks from the new card issuer, the consumer is having a rare experience. However, if this is the case, the consumer may visit any banking institution that displays the Visa or MasterCard logo, request a cash advance, and then purchase a cashier's check for the amount of the existing card's balance. The cashier's check should be made payable to and mailed to the old card issuer.

HIDDEN COSTS OF CREDIT CARDS

Despite laws regarding the disclosure of terms for credit card use, many credit cards have hidden costs. The timing of transactions, payment methods, methods of applying interest rates, the types of balances, and the disposition of the credit card issuer may add to the cost of using a credit card. Unless consumers acquire a credit card issued from a reputable financial institution that has a history of keeping rates low or acquires a credit card issued in Arkansas, there is no guarantee of the cost of using a credit card. State laws that govern credit cards issued in Arkansas were enacted to keep rates low. State laws enacted in states such as Delaware and South Dakota cap interest rates at a reasonable level. However, a 1978 Supreme Court decision provides for nationally chartered banks to export its terms of credit card agreements to states that cap interest rates. While the decision applies to banks, it did not apply to retail stores. A federal law was passed in 1987 to allow retailers to create credit card banks, to export credit card rates under the 1978 Supreme Court decision. In general, the laws that govern the state where a credit card operation is located determine the interest rates that may be charged. Credit card operations that are based in Delaware and South Dakota have interest rates that are capped according to state laws.

Date of Purchase Versus Date of Posting

Credit card issuers may apply interest from the date of purchase or the date of posting. The date of purchase is the date on which the actual transaction between the merchant and the consumer took place. The date of posting is the date on which the charge reaches the card issuer and is placed in a consumer's account. When interest is applied from the date of posting, the period of time for which interest is applied may differ from one to several days less than when the date of purchase is used.

Minimum Payments

Minimum credit card payments have continued to shrink over the years. Some card issuers have minimum payments that are as low as two percent of the card balance. This reduction in minimum payments ensures that consumers who make the minimum payment each month pay a hefty interest over the life of the credit card account. Low minimum payments are a positive when consumers are low on cash, but consumers can always pay more than the minimum and save lots of money in interest in the long run.

Fixed Rates

Fixed rate credit cards differ from the fixed rate loans such as those acquired for mortgages or vehicles. With fixed rate mortgage loans, for example, consumers can be assured that the same interest rate will be applied throughout the life of the loan. Credit cards are advertised to have fixed interest rates, but the law allows card issuers to change interest rates at any time so long as a 15 day notice of the change is given. A new interest rate may then be applied to current balances as well as purchases. The credit card agreement will disclose the true terms of applying interest rates.

Variable Rates

As with mortgages, variable rate credit cards have interest that is tied to some other interest rate in the economy, such as the prime rate that is listed in the Wall Street Journal or the federal discount rate. If these other rates change, the interest rate applied to the credit card account also changes. Card issuers are free to choose how they compute such interest rates. Some may choose to add some percentage to these other rates or have their interest rates duplicate these other rates. Most variable rate credit card issuers change their rates on a quarterly basis and some change semiannually. A card issuer's method of calculating variable rates and the time for which they change the rates must be disclosed in applications and solicitations for the particular credit card. Most variable rate credit cards have "floors" below which the interest will not decrease. Even if the interest rates to which variable rate credit cards are tied fall below the "floor," the variable credit card rate will not decrease below the "floor" level.

Tiered Rates

Tiered rate credit cards have interest rates that are dependent upon the balance of the credit card account. The lowest interest rates are applied to high balances and higher interest rates are applied to low balances. The tiered interest method of rewarding high account balances equates to rewarding cardholders for going deeper into debt.

Type of Balance Based Rates

Many credit cards charge different interest rates dependent upon the type of balance that is held on the account. Low rates, for example, may be applied to balances transferred from other credit cards as part the credit issuer's marketing promotion. Cash advances are an example of a balance that has a high interest rate applied to it. Credit card issuers who charge interest, based on the type of balances on the account, provide their customers with an effective interest rate on their credit card statements. An effective rate is the average of all the different rates that apply to the different types of balance. When cardholders make payment on their credit card accounts, the payment is applied to the lowest rate balance first. This method of paying down low debts first is in direct contrast to all types of debt management which recommend that consumers pay down the highest debts first.

Introductory Rates

Many credit card issuers offer introductory rates as low as zero percent as part marketing and promotion to attract new customers. The issue with introductory rates is that the rates do not remain in effect for too long and are often followed by some of the highest available interest rates. Introductory rates may apply for six months, but if one engages in a balance transfer to take advantage of the offer, the balance transfer may take weeks to complete, thereby shortening the introductory rate to less than six months.

New Issuer Rates

The laws of most states allow card issuers to change interest rates at any time so long as a 15 day notice of the change is given. This is true when one financial institution purchases the credit card accounts of another institution and raises the costs of credit cards. In New York and Delaware, however, state laws require card issuers to provide existing cardholders with a 30 days notice before raising rates, and also requires that card issuers give exiting cardholders an opportunity to pay off the credit card account under the old terms and surrender the credit card.

MANAGE INSURANCE COVERAGE

Insurance coverage is often overlooked when considering those avenues that will assist in maintaining good credit. However, insurance coverage is necessary to protect one's assets, particularly those major purchases that are most cause for debt such as homes. Life and disability insurance also provide financial security for one's family or household in the case of death or injury or illness.

Life Insurance

Life insurance is necessary to cover the contribution that one makes to a family unit in the case of death. Term life insurance is a relatively low cost form of life insurance that covers persons for a specified term. It is usually issued for a specific number of year, and it is usually renewed at the expiration of the initial term. Term life insurance has no cash value or investment value. The value of the policy is paid upon death. It is important to ensure that the coverage amount is enough to supplement the household budget for a reasonable amount of time. The coverage should do more than merely pay for funeral expenses, though such expenses should also be included in determining the amount of coverage needed.

Other forms of life insurance offer cash benefits that the insured party may borrow against. Insured persons are allowed to borrow up to the cash value of the insurance policy. Interest rates on such loans are usually low, and the loans offer their own unique flexibility. The loan does not have to be repaid but should the insured party die before the loan is repaid, the borrowed amount will be deducted from the benefit amount before the proceeds from the benefit amount are distributed to beneficiaries. As such, borrowing against a life insurance policy may defeat the purpose of carrying the insurance and paying premiums.

Disability Insurance

Long-term disability insurance is designed to help cover expenses when one is disabled and unable to work for an extended time. As with any insurance, one must make a reasonable prediction of the amount of necessary coverage and seek a policy that will meet that requirement.

Homeowner's Insurance

Homeowner's insurance is designed to cover a loss to one of the most valuable assets that one will acquire, one's home. Homeowner's insurance coverage should be sufficient to replace the home as well as its contents in the case of a loss. Homeowners must be diligent in keeping up with building code changes, building code requirements, and the affect these changes and requirements will have on replacement costs for a home. Homeowner's insurance may be composed of various types of coverage. It may include coverage for fire, earthquakes, flood, and other natural disasters and perils. Homeowner's insurance should include umbrella coverage for personal and medical liability for injuries on the property. Homeowners should try to establish the highest limits on coverage and the highest deductible that they are comfortable with. The goal is to provide coverage for unexpected incidents that one cannot afford to pay out of pocket. Most mortgage lenders require mortgagees to carry a certain amount of homeowner's insurance as part of the mortgage agreement. While mortgagees may carry more insurance than is required, they may not carry a less amount of insurance.

Car Insurance

Car insurance is required in the United States, and most states also require that a certain amount of liability insurance be acquired for a vehicle to be driven. Liability insurance covers losses that an insured person is liable for when the insured causes an accident. It is required to protect other persons and their property when the insured is at fault or accused of being at fault. Consumers may also purchase personal liability or umbrella insurance coverage that covers liability when the limits of liability insurance have been exhausted. Consumers may also want to purchase collision and comprehensive insurance to protect their own vehicles. Collision insurance covers the insured person's vehicle when the insured is at fault in an accident. Comprehensive insurance covers any other loss or damage to the insured person's vehicle, such as a falling tree. Consumers must first make sure that comprehensive and collision coverage is cost effective when compared to the book value of their vehicles.

WHAT DOES NOT HELP

Some types of credit accounts and financial activities will damage one's credit reputation and should be avoided. Closing accounts, making late payments, having negative information reported in one's credit file, co-signing loans, engaging in suspect lending schemes and engaging in activities that are indications of fraud and identity theft will not help to maintain one's good credit. Consumers need to examine the effects of these types of actions and find ways to avoid them.

Closing Old and Negative Accounts

Closing old accounts may have the negative effect of shortening the life of one's credit history and reducing the mix of healthy credit accounts. If old accounts are closed, consumers should request that the credit file entry indicate that the consumer, not the creditor, closed the account. Closing negative accounts will not remove them from one's credit report. It is best that the consumer pay off the account so that the entry shows that the consumer was able to satisfy the debt.

Late Payments

Payments that are made after the due date, during the grace period, and before a late payment is applied are still late. These types of payments that are generally allowed for mortgages and auto loans and can be reported to credit reporting agencies. When these types of payments are reported to credit reporting agencies as late payments, they may have a negative effect on one's credit score. Attempts to make large payments to make up for missed payments will not improve one's credit score. Even though the large payment makes an account current, the tardiness, when reported, remains a part of one's credit file.

Some lenders will lend money to persons with a history of late payments because these individuals offer profit potential in interest and fees. Other lenders may reject applicants with only one or two late payments in the past 30 days. Some lenders are not so much concerned with the amount that was paid late, but how late the payment was made. As an example, a small late payment amount of $10, which is late by 120 days may do more to hurt an individual's credit rating than a large $1,000 payment, which is only late by 30 days. Other lenders take the amount of the late payment into consideration. For example, some credit scoring methods may ignore collection accounts for less than $250. It is best for consumers to avoid making any late payments.

Negative Marks in Credit Reports

Collection accounts, charge offs, lawsuits, profit-and-loss, judgments, and tax liens are considered negative marks in a credit report. Most lenders and creditors use any negative marks in one's credit report as the basis to reject applications for credit, particularly when those bad marks have not been paid off or they have occurred in the past two years.

Co-signing

Loans that one co-signs for, which are in default, are included in the co-signer's credit file and treated as a debt of the co-signer. Until the debt is satisfied and the legal time for reporting the negative information has passed, the debt remains in the co-signer's credit file.

Auto Equity Loans

Auto equity loans are a scam devised by unscrupulous people who advertise, usually in the classified section of newspapers, to assume vehicle loans for consumers who cannot make their loan payments. This type of advertising is geared toward consumers who are facing repossession and buyers who do not qualify for financing through legitimate lenders.

An auto equity firm purchases vehicles from consumers who cannot make their loan payments and then sells or leases the vehicle to some other person. The seller is led to believe that his or her responsibility for the vehicle has ended. However, the auto equity firm does not really assume the loan on the vehicle with the original lender. In fact, the auto equity firm has no relationship nor does it establish a relationship with the original lender. Instead, the auto equity firm resells the vehicle to a third party, who is required to make payments to the original lender in the form of a certified check or to make payments to the auto equity firm, which in turn will make payment to the original lender.

The original lender is never notified of the transactions because in most instances, the transactions are illegal. Most vehicle loan contract agreements do not allow a consumer to sell, lease, or sublease an unpaid vehicle without notifying the lender. This type of language is purposely put into vehicle loan contracts to protect the original lender's interest until the loan amount is paid in full.

The scams carried out by auto equity lenders may easily create problems for consumers who sell to them, such as the failure to transfer titles and the failure to transfer tags, making the seller responsible for any future problems or acts that involve the vehicle. Further, if the scam falls through and payments are not made to the original lender, the seller remains responsible to pay any outstanding balance on the vehicle loan even though he or she no longer has possession or use of the vehicle.

Consumers who are considering engaging in an auto equity loan should first check with their state motor vehicle administration to ensure that such firms are legal in the state. They must then contact the original lender to find out if the required transactions are permissible. Finally, they should check with the state or local consumer protection agency and the Better Business Bureau to ensure that the company has a good track record for doing business.

Child Support Arrearage

Traditionally, child support arrearage was not a consideration in credit evaluations. However, child support arrearage takes precedence over other types of debt in bankruptcy. As such, more and more lenders look negatively upon the failure to make child support payments because child support debt would have to be satisfied before any credit extended by the lender.

Finance Company Lines of Credit

By virtue of engaging in a loan with a finance company, a consumer is considered a high risk, even if the loan has a history of being paid on time. Traditionally, lenders and creditors considered finance companies to be the lender of last resort. However, many finance companies, particularly large and well-known companies, such as GMAC, are no longer considered companies of last resort. They are recognized for the convenience that they offer to consumers. Consumers who decide to engage a loan with a finance company should be sure to contract with a reputable company.

Finance companies have a reputation for taking on high risk consumers who do not qualify for conventional loans because they are too far in debt. Finance companies assume this risk because they supplement the risk with extremely high interest rates, some as high as 25 percent. They also charge a variety of fees and offer low monthly payments that are affordable to these high-risk borrowers, but more important they assure that the loan has a long life so that the finance company will make large amounts of money in finance charges.

Some finance companies cleverly distort their advertising such that it appears that they are offering debt consolidation loans, which are illegal in most states. They are really offering a home equity loan. This type of home equity loan can be costly with spiraling debt due to the high interest rates and low payment amount. Consumers should engage in home equity loans with a bank or credit union, not a finance company.

Bill Paying Services

Bill paying services can be dangerous since many distort their advertising so that they appear to be offering debt consolidation services. However, bill-paying services do not consolidate debts. What they do is pay a consumer's bills each month, but they do not refinance nor pay off any loans. The consumer provides the service with a single payment each month to be used to pay the consumer's creditors. In addition, the consumer is required to pay the service a monthly or annual fee, which could amount to as much as 10 percent of the consumer's monthly debt. This additional debt does nothing to assist the consumer in paying down debts. In fact, it adds to a consumer's existing debt.

Many bill paying services are not regulated and many have failed to pay consumers' bills on time or gone out of business without contacting the consumer. Most consumers find out that their bill paying service is no longer existent only when they begin to receive notices for their debts from collection agencies. Some states do regulate for-profit bill paying services, and in other states they are illegal. Consumers should be sure to contact their state's attorney general to find out which laws apply in their state before engaging such services.

Payday Loans

Payday loans are a growing market of loans, which are offered through most check cashing businesses. Check cashing businesses were established to cash checks for consumers, particularly those consumers who had no bank account. According to the Consumer Federation of America (CFA), a nonprofit organization, check cashing fees for payroll checks have been known to range from 1 percent to 6 percent of the check amount, with average of 2.34 percent. Personal check fees have ranged from 1.85 percent to 16 percent of the check amount, with an average of about 9.36 percent.

In recent years, these companies have engaged in billions of dollars of transactions through their payday loan services, which provide for consumers to borrow cash over a short period of time (until payday) at outrageous interest rates. Interest rate may be assessed for as much as 1,820 percent. Payday loans are readily available to consumers with bad and no credit history. However, consumers are required to have a checking account in good standing to participate in the loan program. Many of these businesses are not regulated and do not abide by interest ceilings established by state laws. A few states, however, have banned the use of payday loans or capped the amount of costs associated with these types of loans.

Consumers use their personal checks to write a check to the check cashing business. The check cashing business immediately provides the consumer with a large portion of the check amount. As an example, the consumer presents the check cashing business with a check for $150 and immediately receives $125 in cash. The check cashing business agrees to hold the check until the consumer is paid. This may be a matter of days or weeks. Many of these businesses offer their services over the Internet and promise to wire money to their customer's accounts overnight. On payday, the consumer either repays the cash amount that was provided, allows the check cashing business to cash the personal check that it held, or allows the check cashing business to roll over the cash amount that was provided into a new loan to be paid on the next payday. In return for the latter, the consumer must pay an additional fee. Expanding on the example above, the initial fee paid to the check cashing business was $25. To roll over the borrowed amount to the next payday, the consumer is charged an additional fee of $25. When consumers need cash in a hurry, these fees may seem minimal, but they represent a high effective interest rate. The effective interest represents the interest for a loan over the length of time for which the money was borrowed. If the annual interest rate for paying $25 to borrow $125 is 20 percent, the effective interest rate for paying $25 on $125 for one day, five days or two weeks is much more. The CFA found that effective interest rates for seven day loans were as much as 1,820 percent.

Filing Bankruptcy

Many lenders and creditors consider bankruptcy to be the most negative entry that may be included in one's credit report. Even when one files for bankruptcy and does not follow through with the actual proceedings, the fact that one filed will still be reported in their credit file. Debts that are repaid through

Chapter 13 are equally negative to debts discharged through Chapter 7 of the bankruptcy code. Lenders and creditors may reject applications for credit for individuals who have filed for bankruptcy, particularly a recent bankruptcy.

Higher Income

Though income is a large factor used in determining whether to extend credit to an individual, an increase in income or high income will not offset negative entries in one's credit report or the lack of a credit history. Most creditors have an income limit for loans or lines of credit. The requirement may be as little as $10,000 or as high as $35,000 for gold card status. A high or increased income may provide for a higher credit line if one has a good credit history. However, a high income will not compensate for a negative credit history. Most lenders require proof of income. Persons who are self-employed may be required to provide copies of their tax returns or other proof of income. Some lenders will consider the income per dependent and request information about one's dependents.

Pawn Brokers

Pawnbrokers accept merchandise in return for a short term cash loan. These loans usually amount to a small percentage of the actual cash value of the merchandise, and the interest applied to the loan is high with unfavorable terms. If a consumer is not able to pay back the loan on time, the consumer partially reneges on ownership of the merchandise, and the pawnbroker is free to sell the merchandise. If the pawnbroker is able to sell the merchandise for more than it is worth, the original owner of the merchandise is supposed to be paid the difference between the cash value and the sale price. This type of loan should be avoided.

Indications of Fraud

Lenders have identified suspicious activities that may be indicators of identity fraud in filing applications for credit. Many credit reporting agencies, lenders, and creditors make use of fraud detection systems to alert them to information supplied on credit applications that are characteristic of fraud. Consumers are cautioned to provide complete, accurate information on credit applications to avoid being rejected for suspicion of fraud. Some common indicators of application fraud include the following:

Suspicious Addresses.

The use of post office boxes, particularly for those individuals who do not live in rural areas, sends a red flag. Some credit reporting agencies and creditors have systems that seek out addresses of prisons, mail drops, and commercial properties. Creditors may also be alerted to home and work addresses that are the same, zip codes that do not match the address, or work and home addresses that are in different state, particularly if the commuting distance seems unreasonable.

Discrepancies in Social Security Numbers.

Credit reporting agencies and creditors will check to ensure that the social security number provided on an application matches the number held in their files or the number used in other files. They also check to ensure that the number is valid, not that of someone else or someone who is deceased.

Discrepancies in Employer Information.

Though many creditors do not concentrate on employment histories, many do verify employment information. When the employer's address or name cannot be verified, the application raises suspicion. When individuals indicate being hired on dates that correspond to a Saturday, Sunday, or holiday, a red flag is raised.

Inaccurate Bank Account Numbers.

When savings and checking account numbers are incorrectly entered on an application, the applicant raises suspicion. Creditors may verify bank account information for validity and also to ensure that an account was not opened just before applying for credit.

CONCLUSION

To repair your credit score, you must initiate a sequence of actions that will require credit reporting agencies, creditors, debt collectors, and other entities with which you engage in financial transactions to ensure that the information they compile, report, and/or sell about you is accurate. This information is used to calculate your credit score and when it is incorrect, inaccurate, outdated, or wrong it could damage your credit rating and credit score for years beyond its initial entry into your credit file.

Another aspect of repairing your credit score involves understanding credit and how various types of credit may help or harm your credit rating and credit score. You need to evaluate your ability to take advantage of the various credit options and make use of those credit types that will be most beneficial to you at any given time or in any given circumstance. Life events such as graduation, employment, or marriage may affect your ability to obtain or maintain certain types of credit. Your financial and credit histories, as compiled and recorded by credit reporting agencies, may be responsible for improving or damaging your credit rating and credit score if you are not responsible for monitoring the information that is compiled on you and take steps to make sure that it is correct.

You are probably aware of standard credit reports compiled about you that outline your financial history, but there are two types of credit reports that may be purchased about you. A standard credit report is the report that most lenders and creditors purchase. An investigative credit report may also be purchased, which contains more detailed information about your financial history and your behaviors. As if that were not enough, there are also other types of consumer reports that are used to profile your worthiness in other types of transactions that involve money. Insurance companies, employers, and other business entities purchase consumer reports about you that include information other than credit histories. They also purchase scores that are other than credit scores, but relate to the particular area of interest. While these other consumer reports and scores may not directly affect your credit score, they may be used to damage your ability to engage in activities that you thought only your credit score would be used to qualify for.

While there are many factors involved in repairing your credit score, your personal commitment to repairing your score is important. You, not the credit reporting agencies, your creditors, nor the government is going to take responsibility to repair your credit score for you. This book will give you all of the information that you'll need to begin repairing your credit score now.

REFERENCES

1   *Credit Repair Kit For Dummies*

2   *Credit Repair: What the Credit Industry Doesn't Want You to Know*

3   *Pocket Idiot's Guide to Repairing your Credit (The Pocket Idiot's Guide)*

4   *The Complete Credit Repair Kit* (+ CD-ROM) (Complete Credit Repair Kit)

5   *The Everything Personal Finance in Your 20s & 30s Book: Erase Your Debt, Personalize Your Budget and Plan Now to Secure Your Future* (Everything Series)

6   *The Guerrilla Guide to Credit Repair: How to Find out What's Wrong with Your Credit Rating and How to Fix It*

7   *The Ultimate Credit Handbook: How to Cut Your Debt and Have a Lifetime of Great Credit*, Third Edition

8   *Your Credit Score: How to Fix, Improve, and Protect the 3-Digit Number that Shapes Your Financial Future*

AUTHOR BIOGRAPHY & DEDICATION

This book is dedicated to my nieces and nephews: James III, Dominic, Juanai, Myia, Cobin, Winesha, and Nashay.

Jamaine Burrell is a mathematician, analyst, and freelance writer who lives in Baltimore, Maryland. Her combined talents have led to the authorship of this book as well as other small business and real estate books under the Atlantic Publishing Group.

GLOSSARY

Learning credit terminology can be daunting. If you are investigating credit options and want to know what is involved, use this guide to understand the more common credit terms.

ACCION Adapted the CAMEL (see CAMEL) instrument to the micro finance industry as a quantitative and qualitative assessment of MFI financial performance.

Active Clients The number of borrowers who have loans outstanding on the date a lending institution's financial statements are filed.

Active Loan Portfolio All money that is "on the street" or owed to a lender on the date financial reports are filed. The total amount of repaid loans is higher than the total amount loaned out.

Adjustable rate mortgage A mortgage with an interest rate that will rise, dependent on influences such as interest rates on Treasury securities.

Adjusted Balance An advantage to borrowers and credit card holders. A way of calculating your credit balance and annual percentage rate (APR) when payments and/ or credits made during the billing cycle are subtracted from the borrower's balance at the end of the previous billing cycle. Unlike average daily balance calculations, interest is only applied to the balance remaining after payments are credited to your account, and new purchases during that billing cycle are not included in adjusted balance calculations.

Adverse Action Any negative action taken as a result of information in your consumer report.

Affinity card A credit card that makes a donation to a charity of your choice based on how much you spend, usually with a higher interest rate than normal.

Amortization Amortization is a payment plan that allows the borrower to reduce his/her debt through monthly payments of principal. The process of fully paying off a debt by installments over a fixed time.

Annual Percentage Rate (APR) A measure of how much interest will be charged a borrower; also called the cost of credit. The rate cannot be changed after a lending contract is signed unless stated upfront.

Application scoring The use of a formula to "score" credit applications and credit bureau data to decide whether to grant a loan.

Appraisal An estimate of the value of real estate by a professional appraiser.

ATM (Automated Teller Machine) A cash machine. Used to withdraw money direct from your credit card, although in general a fee will also be charged.

Automatic Stay Bankruptcy courts impose a stay to prevent creditors from taking collection actions against the debtor.

Average Daily Balance A daily tracking of what you owe by calculating your credit balance and interest and then crediting your account from the day your payment is received. New purchases will not necessarily be added on the day of the purchase and will not show in your daily balance.

Balloon loan A short-term fixed rate loan involving low payments for a set period of time, ending with a large payment for the unpaid principal at a time specified in the contract.

Bankruptcy A form of financial protection in which the borrower is unable to pay rent or mortgage payments, has no credit or means of paying for it, and is unable to reconcile with collection agencies. This proceeding in U.S. Bankruptcy Court may legally release a person from repaying debts owed. Credit reports normally include bankruptcies for up to 10 years. The two methods of filing for personal bankruptcy are Chapter 7 and Chapter 13. A Chapter 7 bankruptcy eliminates all debts (except taxes) by taking all non-exempt property and converting it to cash to pay off debts. A Chapter 13 bankruptcy allows a borrower with a steady income to pay off bills over a 36-to 60-month period.

Budget A detailed plan for income and expenditures during a specific period of time.

Buy down A lump-sum payment made to the creditor by the borrower or by a third party to reduce some or all of the consumer's debt.

CAMEL A U.S. Federal Reserve-developed diagnostic tool that rates financial institutions' capital assets, management, earnings, and liquidity.

Charge-off A loan written off as a bad debt.

Closing costs Any appraiser fees, points paid, or other miscellaneous fees added to a loan, not including interest.

Collection A collection department or agency's attempted recovery of a past-due credit obligation.

Consumer credit file   A credit bureau record on a given individual.

Consumer finance   Refers to any kind of lending to consumers.

Credit bureau   The three largest credit bureaus in the United States are Equifax, Experian, and TransUnion. They are credit reporting agencies for information on individuals' or firms' credit rating.

Credit bureau risk score   A score based solely on data stored at the major credit bureaus.

Credit Card   Card authorizing the account holder to charge purchases against a pre-approved credit line, issued by banks, thrift institutions, retailers, and gasoline companies, for example. Many card issuers charge an annual fee to cover account servicing costs. Credit card purchases normally become payable after a grace period (up to 30 days) during which no finance charge is imposed. Credit card interest rates, annual fees, and repayment terms vary considerably.

Credit history   A record of how promptly a consumer has repaid credit obligations.

Credit obligation   An agreement by which a person is legally bound to pay back borrowed money or used credit.

Credit Opportunity Act (ECOA)   Federal legislation of 1974 (Title VII of the Consumer Credit Protection Act) that prohibits discrimination in credit.

Credit report   Information communicated by a credit reporting agency that relates to a consumer's credit standing.

Credit risk   Likelihood that an individual will pay his or her credit obligations as agreed.

Credit score Credit bureau risk scores.

Credit Union A nonprofit, cooperative financial institution owned and run by its members.

Debt Load Total amount of money a consumer owes.

Debt-to-income ratio A comparison of gross income to housing and non-housing expenses; with the FHA, the-monthly mortgage payment should be no more than 29 percent of monthly gross income (before taxes) and the mortgage payment combined with non-housing debts should not exceed 41 percent of income.

Default Failure to make a loan or debt payment when due.

Delinquent A failure to deliver even the minimum payment on a loan or debt payment on or before the time agreed.

Development Finance Term that encompasses all financial services provided to low-income clientele in less developed nations, including micro loans, micro savings, and micro insurance.

Dischargeable Debt A debt that can be eliminated in bankruptcy.

Down payment Amount to be paid up front rather than financed.

Economic index Major economic components such as wholesale prices, housing starts, and inflation that are averaged and used to measure economic health.

Economic indicator Key statistics that reveal the direction of the economy, for example, the unemployment rate and the inflation rate.

Escrow Property or money held by a third party until obligations of a contract are met. For example, real estate taxes may be added to a loan payment and paid by the lender.

Fair Credit Reporting Act (FCRA)   Federal legislation of 1970 that prohibits improper use of information in the files of consumer reporting agencies.

Fair Debt Collection Practices Act (FDCPA)   A federal law prohibiting abusive and unfair debt collection practices.

Fair Isaac Corporation NYSE   Founded in 1956 by engineer Bill Fair and mathematician Earl Isaac, Fair Isaac Corporation NYSE: They developed FICO scores, the most used credit scores in the world.

Fair-Share   A voluntary contribution from creditor.

FICO® scores   Credit bureau risk scores produced from models developed by Fair Isaac Corporation are commonly known as FICO scores.

Fixed rate   An interest rate that does not change during the term of the loan.

Foreclosure   Refers to the lender's legal action to take possession of real property used to secure repayment for a loan when a debtor defaults.

Furnisher of information   Anyone who provides information about anyone to a credit reporting agency for a credit report. A credit card company, landlord, collection agency, and mortgage companies are all furnishers of information.

Grace Period   Number of days between the time a credit card bill is sent and when the payment is due without incurring interest charges.

Home equity line of credit (HELOC)   A mortgage loan that allows the borrower to obtain multiple advances of the loan proceeds at his or her discretion, up to a percentage of the borrower's equity in the property.

Indirect finance Means borrowing funds from the financial market through, for example, a financial intermediary. This is different from direct financing where there is a direct connection to the financial markets as indicated by the borrower issuing securities directly on the market. Common methods for direct financing include a financial auction where price of the security is bid upon or an initial public offering where the security is sold for a set initial price.

Inquiry An item on a consumer's credit report that shows that someone has previously requested a copy of the consumer's report. Fair Isaac credit bureau risk scores count only inquiries resulting from a consumer's application for credit.

Installment credit Loan repaid in equal periodic payments of principal and interest.

Installment debt Most mortgage and auto loans debts, which are to be paid at regular times over a specified period.

Insurance Number of days that insurance coverage is in force although premiums have not been paid.

Insurance bureau score Based solely on credit bureau data, it offers a snapshot of an individual's insurance risk, used to evaluate auto and homeowner insurance policies.

Interest A fee charged for the use of money.

Interest A percentage charged to the amount owed when borrowing money.

Interest rate Percent of interest charged on a loan payment.

Introductory (or intro) rate   Low rate charged by a lender for an initial period after which the rate charged increases.

Judgment   A legal decision; when requiring debt repayment, it may apply a property lien to secure the creditor's claim by providing a source of collateral.

KOBA code   A one- or two-alpha code to define the industry or type of service a given company offers.

Late payment   A delinquent payment; a failure to deliver a loan or debt payment on or before the time agreed.

Lender   A person or company that loans money for a given period of time.

Liquidation   The process of converting assets into cash.

Loan   Borrowed money, usually repaid with interest.

Major purchase   A purchase for a substantial amount of money: a car or home.

Manner of Payment (MOP)   A series of codes or statements used to show a consumer's payment habits.

Medium high-risk   Medium high-risk consumers may have had delinquencies, charge-offs or public record items; they will most likely pay high interest rates because of their risk level.

Medium low-risk   Medium low risk consumers have generally exhibited responsible credit behavior. They may have one or two delinquencies on their credit report.

Medium risk   Medium risk consumers' credit reports have one or more delinquencies, high outstanding debt or relatively new credit accounts. Such consumers are usually able to obtain credit but at higher interest rates.

Member summary (record)
A subset of **ConsumerInfo. com**, Inc., an Experian company file containing all relevant data about each member. A minimum amount of information is maintained on each member, including contact information.

Micro credit A part of the field of micro finance, it is the provision of credit services to low-income entrepreneurs.

Micro enterprise A small-scale business in the informal sector. They employ fewer than five people and can be based out of the home.

Micro entrepreneur
Proprietor of a micro enterprise.

Micro finance Financial services targeted to low- and moderate-income businesses or households including the provision of credit.

Micro finance Institution
(MFI) A financial institution that provides micro finance products and services to low-income clients.

Micro insurance A developing field of micro finance that provides health insurance and other insurance products to micro entrepreneurs.

Micro loan A loan from a micro finance institution to a micro entrepreneur to develop the borrower's small business. They are used to purchase goods for the micro enterprise, as capital for construction, or in the purchase of fixed assets that aid in production, among other things.

Mortgage brokers Trained professionals who search for the best loan rates for borrowers, working as a liaison between banks and borrowers.

National Foundation for Consumer Credit Nonprofit organization that educates consumers about using credit wisely. It is the parent group of Consumer Credit Counseling Service.

Non-dischargeable Debt A debt that cannot be eliminated in bankruptcy.

Obsolescence The term used to describe how long negative information should stay in a credit file before it is no longer considered relevant to the credit granting decision. The FCRA has determined the obsolescence period to be ten years in the case of bankruptcy and seven years in all other instances.

Paid as Agreed An item on the credit report showing that the consumer repaid the credit account according to the terms of the loan.

PMI payment Private Mortgage Insurance (PMI). For home loans secured with less than 20 percent down, PMI is commonly added to insure the lending institution. It is removed at your request when equity exceeds 20 percent of the original purchase price.

Points The total units of prepaid interest used to reduce the interest rate of your mortgage. Each point equals 1 percent of your mortgage balance.

Principal The amount owed on a loan, minus interest. Rate cap The maximum amount an adjustable rate mortgage interest rate can increase in one year.

Re-age To update an account status as current when the account is delinquent.

Real estate agent A person trained and licensed to deal with the purchase, sale, and marketing of real estate property.

Refinancing To take out a new mortgage on the same property, typically at a lower rate.

Repossession If you purchase an item on credit and fail to pay for it, the entity that sold it to you reclaims or repossesses it.

Retail Banking According to **investopedia.com**, retail banking is mass-market banking involving local branches of larger commercial banks. Services include savings and checking accounts, mortgages, personal loans, debit cards, and credit cards.

Retail banks –

• **Commercial bank** is the term used for a normal bank to distinguish it from an investment bank. Some use the term for a bank that deals with or large businesses.

• **Community development banks** provide financial services and credit to underserved markets or populations.

• **Private banks** manage assets of high net worth individuals.

• **Offshore banks** are located in countries with low taxation and regulation. They are essentially private banks.

• **Savings banks** accept savings deposits.

Revolving Account –Requires a minimum payment each month in addition to a service charge. When the balance

decreases, the service charge/ interest also declines.

Postal savings banks are associated with national postal systems.

Revolving credit Credit repeatedly available up to a specified amount as periodic repayments are made.

Revolving debt Debt owed on an account that the borrower can repeatedly use and pay back without having to reapply every time credit is used. Credit cards are the most common type of revolving account.

Sales price   Total price for an item, including taxes and fees. Sales tax   Total amount of sales tax on a purchase.

Savings Mobilization Programs intending to mobilize the capital of the poor and to provide savings accounts, as well as credit services, to micro entrepreneurs and low-income households.

Score   See "credit score."

Scorex   One of the world's leading decision solutions and business intelligence organizations, using data mining and analysis, scoring models, market analysis, and business intelligence. The company has offices in 26 countries supporting clients in over 50 countries worldwide.

Scoring model   A statistical formula used to estimate future performance of prospective borrowers and existing customers. It is based on a consumer's credit report.

Small and Medium Scale Enterprises (SMEs) Companies employing five to ten workers (small-scale) or between 10 and 50 workers (medium-scale).

Stepped Lending Arrangements by which borrowers who repay loans on time are eligible for increasingly larger loans.

Sub-prime   Describes customers who are bad credit risks, but are considered for loans because the increased risk allows the finance company to charge higher fees.

Subsidized Rates of Interest   Often subsidized by donations, low loan interest rates offered by lending institutions.

Term   Length of time for paying back a loan.

Third-party collectors Collection agencies.

Time-Barred Debt   Old debts that are beyond the point at which a creditor or debt collector can sue you to collect.

Total closing costs Amount of upfront costs paid such as a loan origination fee and any points.

Tradeline   Any credit account such as a bank loan, credit card, or mortgage.

Truth in Lending Act   Title I of the Consumer Protection Act requires lenders to disclose the annual interest rate, the total dollar cost, and other terms of loans and credit sales.

Unsecured Loans Defined Unsecured loans are not guaranteed with any asset; thus, the risk of repossession does not exist.

Village banking   Lending methodology in which clients usually women   form groups of about 10-30 people who are responsible for leadership, bylaws, bookkeeping, fund management, and loan supervision. The group pools funds to use for business loans, savings, and mutual support, and members cross-guarantee individual loans.

INDEX